ROGER'S WORLD

ROGER'S WORLD

The Life and Unusual Times of Roger Neilson

WAYNE SCANLAN

Library and Archives Canada Cataloguing in Publication

Scanlan, Wayne
Roger's world : the life and unusual times of Roger Neilson /
Wayne Scanlan.

Includes index.
ISBN 0-7710-7962-1

1. Neilson, Roger, 1934-2003. 2. Hockey coaches – Biography. 3. Hockey – Canada – Biography. 4. Hockey – United States – Biography. I. Title.

GV848.5.N43S32 2004 796.962'092 C2004-903854-0

We acknowledge the financial support of the Government of Canada through the Book Publishing Industry Development Program and that of the Government of Ontario through the Ontario Media Development Corporation's Ontario Book Initiative. We further acknowledge the support of the Canada Council for the Arts and the Ontario Arts Council for our publishing program.

Typeset in Sabon by M&S, Toronto
Printed and bound in Canada

This book is printed on acid-free paper that is
100% ancient forest friendly (100% post-consumer recycled).

McClelland & Stewart Ltd.
The Canadian Publishers
481 University Avenue
Toronto, Ontario
M5G 2E9
www.mcclelland.com

1 2 3 4 5 08 07 06 05 04

For Clare Scanlan, who shared Roger's belief
in God and love of baseball

And for Bern Scanlan, who keeps surprising us

Contents

Foreword

It was 1962 that I first met Roger Neilson. I was working with the Montreal Canadiens as their head scout for eastern Canada.

I'd coached junior hockey in Peterborough with the Petes for three years, beginning in 1958, and the Canadiens, Peterborough's parent team, had an opening for a scout. I was single at the time and based in Ottawa, boarding with a family.

In those days, there was no draft; NHL teams were affiliated with particular clubs, so you looked at young kids when they were midget age. Once you had them in junior, you had their amateur rights and their professional rights. I believe it was in the fall of '62 I hired Roger – to scout the Toronto Hockey League (THL) for us. There were a lot of good players there. Roger was coaching a team called Bick's Pickles, a midget THL club, and he was also coaching a Junior B team in Aurora at the same time.

The arena manager there was a guy named Ernie Batson, and he'd been a scout with Montreal. He was a bird dog, and I'm pretty sure it was Ernie who introduced me to Roger. So we met, and I couldn't offer him much money, but he was also teaching in north Toronto and operating a large newspaper route.

The odd time he'd let his assistant coach the Aurora club if his midget team was playing at the same time, but it didn't happen too often. And he was coaching baseball all summer. He

was the busiest guy I ever met, always going somewhere, always doing something, always something ahead of him.

For me to contact him, there was a window of about fifteen minutes in the morning, between 7:15 and 7:30, when he was usually at home. After he did his morning paper route, he would have a shower, and then he was on his way to school. If I caught him before he left, we could talk for about ten minutes, about players and that sort of thing. Sometimes I'd miss him and I'd get his mother on the phone.

Whenever I was in Toronto, I'd watch his midget team play. He had some kids make Junior A and beyond. Brian Glennie played for him, and so did Rocky Farr, a goalie who played a few seasons in Buffalo.

A job with the Peterborough Petes came open in the fall of 1966, and we met with Sam Pollock, the Canadiens general manager, about Roger taking the position. At first he was in player personnel, then he filled in as coach and stayed on. We drafted Bob Gainey of the Petes in 1973, and Roger was instrumental in that. There were a lot of kids in the league with better numbers – Gainey only had 22 goals in his final year of junior – but Roger was very high on him.

At that time, we were looking for a good defensive player, so we took Gainey eighth overall, and obviously that worked out pretty well.

Then there was Doug Jarvis. The Houston Aeros of the World Hockey Association had drafted him, and the Toronto Maple Leafs drafted him in the second round in 1975, but I remember Roger saying that Jarvis was "the best faceoff man in hockey."

I said, "You mean junior."

And he said, "I'd put him up against anybody in hockey."

This was in 1975, and Bobby Clarke had just eaten everybody up on faceoffs during the playoffs. We had a defenceman

named Greg Hubick; Toronto wanted him and we didn't, so we talked to the Leafs about taking him for Jarvis. Roger said, "You better do that deal quickly, because he'll be going to Houston." So, we traded Hubick for Jarvis, and he signed with us. (Jarvis played 964 consecutive games in the NHL, a record that has stood for seventeen seasons. Hubick played seventy-seven NHL games.)

We had some injuries in Montreal, so Jarvis joined us right away and didn't play a single game in the minors.

Roger went to Dallas shortly after that, hired by the Leafs and Chicago Blackhawks for an opening they had in the AHL. That was a big decision for him to leave Peterborough. I don't think he had any great desire to be involved in pro sports.

And then, of course, he went to the Leafs.

When I left Montreal to go to Buffalo as general manager and head coach, Roger was the first person I called. I hired him to be my assistant. We did well; the team went from seventh overall to second. We reached the Wales Conference finals, but we had a nine-day layoff going in because we swept Chicago in the semifinals. That was just too long. The New York Islanders were ready and we were rusty.

Roger became head coach the next season, as we had planned. We slipped a little that year, and Buffalo management was on me a bit. I knew he was a good coach, and we had to either buy out his contract or keep him. We parted ways, and he had an opportunity in Vancouver.

We had some battles. I was the opposite of Roger. He was very non-confrontational. He was like "Badger" Bob Johnson that way. It just wasn't Roger's style to get after people. He was in education, was groomed as a teacher, so I think his attitude was to reason with players, encourage them. He wouldn't confront a player, but I remember he didn't like Rick Martin, because Rick didn't like to work much at practice.

Like any two people, we had some disagreements, but never to the point where I couldn't pick up the phone and call him. He liked defensive players, and Buffalo ownership was trying to come down on me, saying we didn't play "the right kind of hockey." I said, "Well, we're doing pretty well."

So we decided to have a meeting. And this was pretty funny, because we were sitting around the table with the Knox brothers and Bob Swados and Dave Forman. There were about fifty people who owned that team.

The Knoxes were talking, mostly to me, about our style of play. They wanted to be able to attract more fans, and the economy wasn't strong. So they looked over at Roger, and he was sound asleep at the table.

They were trying to tell us our hockey wasn't exciting, and the coach was asleep.

Roger had his dog Mike with him in Buffalo, and he kept him in his office. Some people didn't like that. I know he was different, but he was a hard worker and a good coach and had good connections.

He was especially strong as a teacher, excellent one-on-one with players. And he was a good bench coach.

He'll be remembered for his innovations. Some of them worked, some didn't. But his players never got tired of him, because he was not afraid to try new things.

And he was ultra-organized. Roger could've been a draftsman or an architect. He was always writing things down, making lists, doing up plans. He reminded me of a baseball manager; he was proactive with his strategy, not reactive.

He was in good shape himself and demanded strong conditioning from his players.

We shared some of the same ideas. We both understood that scoring chances meant a lot more than shots, and that chances were useful in analyzing the game. And what's especially important is the number of scoring chances allowed to the other team.

We both liked matching lines, but Roger's philosophy was different. I liked to match line for line. He was more concerned with getting tired guys off the ice and having fresh guys out there against their tired guys. And he always developed players who could shut down the other team's top line.

Bob Pulford used to say Roger was a better talent scout than he was a coach. I don't know about that; he was a good coach. But he loved to watch hockey. He knew all the players' tendencies, and he would talk to people about players.

He was a background guy, didn't really like being in the forefront.

He was a very smart guy, stubborn, but not to the point that he was unreasonable. He wasn't a guy who would win at all costs, yet he was competitive.

The way I would describe Roger is that he was able to juggle so many balls in the air and he never dropped one.

Scotty Bowman

Scotty Bowman won ten Stanley Cups, nine as a head coach. He went out on top, retiring after leading the Detroit Red Wings to the 2002 Stanley Cup.

Introduction

For two days, friends and admirers by the thousands filed into a hilltop church in Peterborough to pay respects to a man who professed to have no living family.

They laughed through tears – this eclectic mix of the hockey elite and families from down the street – at the endless stories of a coach they knew by a single name: Roger.

Roger Neilson was hockey's foremost innovator. A Hockey Hall of Fame inductee. A member of the Order of Canada. And he was so much more than a hockey coach.

You think you know a public figure like Roger, instructor and mentor to legions of players and coaches. It turns out, people who really thought they knew him continue to make discoveries about this unusual character, this man of character.

Veteran defenceman Dallas Eakins, whose professional career has taken him to twenty stops in the NHL and AHL, would speak with Roger two or three times a week from wherever Eakins was playing to wherever Roger was coaching.

Eakins knew Roger for twenty years, grew up in the Peterborough Petes tradition and was part of the core Neilson hockey-camp group that Roger took to Hawaii every summer. Eakins thought he held a unique place in the man's heart. And he did. He truly did.

It just doesn't feel that way when he talks to others in Roger's world, hears the testimonials from dozens of people who were

inspired by Roger, named babies after him, asked him to be best man at their wedding, godfather to their children.

"If you had asked me three years ago," says Eakins, "I would have said that I knew him better than anyone. And then I find out there's two thousand other people who feel the same way. It's un-believable how stupid I was. You feel like giving yourself a slap – it's amazing how many people were best of friends with Roger."

Dallas Eakins is being a little hard on himself. Given his hockey job, most recently in Vancouver and Winnipeg, and his places of residence, Vancouver and Arizona, Eakins wasn't around Roger enough during the season to know that he spent most of his spare time being an important figure in so many other lives.

You think you know a guy. A hockey guy. Spends his life chal-lenging conventional rules, creating innovative wrinkles such as video analysis, breaks the game down into the components every coach now takes for granted: faceoff percentages, special-team success rates, giveaways, chances. And then you find out he was a baseball manager trapped in a hockey coach's body.

Neilson considered himself blessed to have had a long and storied career in a game he loved – then you find out he loved it second best. Baseball was the sport that Neilson should have been in, and was in for two decades until he was offered a pro hockey contract in 1976. If Neilson had been born in Syracuse, New York, instead of Toronto, Ontario, we might be talking today about "Roger Ball" along with the "Billy Ball" of the late Billy Martin.

Neilson loved the input of a baseball manager: flashing signs, stealing bases, fooling fielders with a hidden apple trick.

Imagine if he'd been in a dugout that night in 1982 and reached for a baseball bat instead of a hockey stick to deliver the universal sign of surrender to the officials. Waving white towels might be a big hit at major-league ballparks today, instead of in NHL arenas.

Neilson was famous in hockey, famous in Canada, but lesser known outside the core American hockey cities.

"His dream job was to be a major-league manager," says Eakins. "Think about Roger's life and career if he were a baseball manager or football coach – his story would be all across North America."

It's a story worth telling.

You think you know a guy. Coached 1,000 NHL games. Had a knack for taking underdog, working-class teams and making them special. So special, they kept getting him fired by overreaching and then making the coach look bad when they eventually found their level.

You think you know a guy. He's nicknamed "Captain Video" for being on the cutting edge of hockey technology in the 1970s. Then you learn that Captain Video is computer illiterate, digital-phobic, and tried to change a television channel with his calculator.

You learn there's this dichotomy running through Roger's life.

Captain Video can't set his VCR.

A thinking man's genius who gets lost in a three-car parade to the airport.

A control freak who empowers his players, dozens of whom call him their favourite coach.

A man nearly as funny as W.C. Fields but who, unlike W.C., adores dogs and children.

Maniacally driven at work, but also driven to play – barefoot. A free spirit under a weathered ball cap.

Roger enjoyed what Ron Smith, one of his assistant coaches, called a Pollyanna existence.

He said he was married to hockey, but had a true love he came close to marrying two or three times.

You think you know a guy. Until you find out he read his Bible the way most coaches read their sports pages. Daily. Occasionally spilling Tim Hortons coffee on the contents.

Above all else, Roger Neilson had this incredible gift of being able to speak with people, especially young people, and leave an impression that would last a lifetime.

He was humble. It was all he could do to say "I." It was always "we." "As a coach, hopefully we've been able to do that," he'd say.

He was caring, to the point that the day before he died, so weak he could barely speak, Roger called his friend Susan Pearce to ask how *she* was doing.

He wasn't afraid to seek opinions on an issue, wasn't reluctant to share hockey knowledge with others. To the contrary, Neilson's coaching clinics were designed to further the game and promote excellence in the profession.

"I often wondered if team owners ever begrudged his sharing of information," says Al Dunford, Neilson's statistician, travel secretary, and travel companion in his days with the Toronto Maple Leafs. "So many coaches around today are his creation; they coach based on his approach and knowledge of the game. With Roger gone, I believe there will be a real deficit in new knowledge of the game."

Camp Without Roger

LINDSAY, Ont. – Only the camp managers, the counsellors, and the rink rats can sense the difference.

They know the significance of the empty gondola seat, mark the unusual quiet, save for the normal sounds of children playing hockey in a camp scrimmage: the sounds of pucks, sticks, skates, and good-natured teasing.

For the more-balanced members of the local population, this is no time to be indoors. It's a steaming July afternoon in a central Ontario town in the heart of the cottage district of the Kawartha Lakes. Just a few miles up the road, at Lock 33 of the vast Trent-Severn Waterway, boaters are busily preparing their crafts for a weekend of activity on Sturgeon Lake and beyond.

Oblivious, at least for the moment, to the pleasures of the outside world, a couple of dozen hockey keeners – some wearing hockey sweaters with nicknames like "Marshmallow," "Tiny

Tiger," "Hit Me," and "Sponge Bob" on the back – are showing off for their parents at the double rinks of the Lindsay Recreation Complex.

Out on the hot concrete beyond the arena parking lot, skateboarders perform a monotonous dance up and down ramps shaped like geometry puzzles. They skate infrequently, active just beyond the point of loitering, and the periodic visits by police remind a visitor of the old saw about idleness and a certain demon's workshop.

In sharp contrast, inside, in the frigid air of the twin ice surfaces, the action is heating up. Another weekly camp session is concluding, which means the usual mixture of emotional farewells, physical exhaustion, dirty laundry, and no small amount of TGIF relief for the directors who make the camp sing.

At the moment, the camp leaders are caught up in emotions quite separate from the standard Friday farewells. And yet it's the quaint trappings of the wrap-up ceremonies that remind them of their burden.

For twenty-six years, along with his role as chief administrator, Roger Neilson would sit in the arena gondola and call the play-by-play of the tournament scrimmages at the hockey camp that bears his name.

He was no threat to take Bob Cole's job on *Hockey Night in Canada,* but it was one of the Roger touches that made this experience different from any other residential hockey camp. In his later years, sick with cancer and prone to the arena chill, Roger set up camp in the gondola. Sitting within range of a portable heater, he would busily scrawl on his omnipresent notepapers – things to do, things to improve.

Many are the camp hockey instructors who looked up from ice level, saw Roger's head buried in his work, and figured they could get away with skipping a particular detail of a particular drill, only to hear from Roger, later, that he'd caught him in the

act. If Roger Neilson didn't have eyes on the top of his famed Abercrombie & Fitch cap, it seemed so.

A tape of Roger's play-by-play of the kids in action was one of the feature presentations at the Friday awards assembly. This week's campers, dressed in their team sweaters, Canadiens and Kings, storm into the campus auditorium of Sir Sandford Fleming College like college football players onto the field of play, to the applause of the parents who have come to take them home.

These are mostly Canadian players of various skill levels between the ages of eight and sixteen, but they also hail from the United States, France, Brazil, Italy, South Korea, and Israel, the latter nation especially a reminder of Roger's broad scope of travel and connections. The awards session begins, as always, with the national anthem, a version sung by Lauren Hart of Philadelphia, Roger's favourite anthem singer.

For insiders, the anthem was a cue. A tug at the heart.

"After the national anthem, it was my time to introduce Rog," says Dave "Ap" Clements, a camp supervisor and a long-time member of the far-flung gang known as Roger's Boys.

"That was kind of a tough moment," says Ap. "All of a sudden, he's not there."

Except in spirit, of course. And on the auditorium screen a video tribute to Roger's career as a hockey coach: 1,000 NHL games as a head coach, a twenty-six-year-run as a head coach or assistant with ten NHL organizations. The presentation includes a clip of Roger delivering his 2002 Hall of Fame induction speech, where he talks of the thrill a little boy once knew at meeting Ted "Teeder" Kennedy of the Maple Leafs.

"Even at eight," Roger says, with a sheepish smirk, "I liked the checkers, I guess."

"You don't want to dwell on the fact he's not here," says Clements to this visitor, regarding the brief public salute to Roger, "but you want to let families know what he stood for."

Larry Pearson, another of the camp supervisors and the executor of Neilson's estate, presents team awards in such categories as character, discipline, and sportsmanship. In the great Neilson tradition, before Pearson is finished, every child has his hands on some kind of souvenir, from a puck to a T-shirt to an NHL game program.

Neilson resembled a bloodhound when it came to sniffing out hockey merchandise he could hand out at his camps. He didn't mind using his clout and charm to lean on NHL players to do their part. "I'm sure he touched them up all year for stuff," says camp director Paul Bedford. "He always had a prize table at the end of camp, to give away gloves, skates, jackets. Two years ago, he freaked everybody out when he gave away all his hockey jackets. It was eerie. Like he figured he wasn't gonna be around."

In the interest of preserving some of the more personal Roger memorabilia, his camp friends snapped up five of his leather hockey jackets and whisked one of them off to the Hockey Hall of Fame.

Habitually, Roger sent the children home with more than trinkets and warm memories of a week of hockey and dry-land-training games. He always had a personal message, one that their parents were likely to remember even if the kids forgot.

Now it's Pearson's turn to deliver the wishes Roger himself would have voiced. It is what he and Bedford, Clements, and fellow supervisor Jim Faulkner have practised in all five weeks of the residential camp: pinch-hitting for Roger. The four have been around Roger's camps for years, know his every trick and command, and still their task is impossible: filling the void left by Roger.

"Be the best you can be, in sports, at school, and at home for your moms and dads," Pearson tells the gathered audience, just before another round of awards: mini-stick this time.

"Go back to your team understanding that it's amazing what a team can accomplish if you don't really care who gets the credit."

The awards ceremony ends, and dozens of campers and their families stream out of the theatre to sort through the batches of

camp souvenirs spread out on tables in the foyer. Each camper automatically receives a send-off package that includes the latest edition of *The Hockey News,* a camp photo, a camp highlight video, and a prize item.

Pearson will admit later how difficult it was to stand up and talk on that first awards night on behalf of Roger, without Roger, and, as Pearson put it, "right after watching that video tribute and he's talking there and looking good, sounding good."

The Peterborough-area cronies who run Neilson's camp – Pearson, Bedford, Clements, Faulkner, Dave Bowen, and Marshall Starkman – wondered if they should hold the camp at all, a twenty-four-hour, five-week, frenetic bit of business that serves more than eight hundred players over five weeks and has to be seen up close to be believed.

Consider the circumstances. Neilson succumbed to cancer on June 21, 2003, coinciding with the NHL entry draft, an event that he loved to avoid. On June 27 and 28, thousands of mourners gathered in Peterborough for a full day of visitation and a memorial service the following day at Northview Pentecostal Church. The next morning, the camp staff were scheduled to begin the mammoth task of opening the first Roger Neilson Hockey Camp without Roger Neilson.

"It started so soon after his death, it's just been a whirlwind," says Starkman, the manager of camp operations and a goaltending instructor. "In many ways, it still hasn't sunk in. We were in the dressing room yesterday and they were showing the ESPY Awards on TV. They mentioned Roger in a tribute to people who had passed away in the past year – and the room sort of went silent. I'm not sure anybody has had time yet to sit back and let this sink in."

Neilson left his school and a junior hockey team he owned in the hands of the four long-time friends – Bedford, Pearson, Clements, and Faulkner – who have always been a part of both enterprises. The four were taught by Neilson at Peterborough's

Crestwood Secondary School in the 1960s and have since become schoolteachers in his likeness.

They pulled into the arena parking lot on the Sir Sandford Fleming College campus, some noticing, some too familiar with it to notice, the arena sign: "Lindsay Recreation Complex, Home of the World Famous Roger Neilson Hockey Camp and Jr. A Lindsay Muskies."

Neilson bought the Muskies of the Ontario Hockey Association in 1996 for $35,000, more or less stumbling into the enterprise when he was inquiring one year about ice time for his camp. He got his Peterborough cronies to run the organization. From wherever Roger's NHL teams were playing on a given night, Neilson would call the Muskies office between periods with two quick questions high on the agenda of any owner: "What's the score . . . and how's the crowd?"

In February, as part of its day-long "Hockey Day in Canada" broadcast, *Hockey Night in Canada* sent its cameras to Lindsay to talk to members of the Muskies operation. Roger would have wanted his twin hockey enterprises, the camp and the OHA Muskies, to soldier on without him. Or would he? In an estate made complicated by his nomadic coaching life, Neilson generously provided for his closest friends and loved ones. He also left 30 per cent of his worth – in excess of three million dollars – to charities, including thirty church groups. Roger could have been a lot richer had he not constantly supported charities in a major way.

Quite pointedly, he did not leave funds for his hockey school or Junior A hockey team, believing they should stand on their own. It's also likely he wanted his friends and business partners to avoid feeling pressured to continue operating the camp and junior club in his absence.

"He made it clear," says Bedford, "it was left up to us."

Because his illness was a long one, Neilson was able to plan for a future that didn't include him. Bedford, who doubled as

camp director and Muskies general manager and head coach, remembers asking Roger if he wanted the hockey school and Muskies to go forward.

"What the crap do I care?" Roger grumbled. "I won't be around." Then he paused for a moment and reconsidered. "Well, it would be nice, because they've been in the family." His extended hockey family, that is. Roger always said he was not aware of having any surviving close relatives.

The foursome entrusted with Roger's estate would carry the camp and Junior A club through to July 8, 2004, when both operations were put up for sale. Roger's friends said they would continue to run the Neilson coaches' clinic in Windsor and hoped to stay on to manage the hockey camp and Muskies team, depending on the wishes of the new owner.

Former students, former players, coaching brethren, and children of all of the above have come to participate in Roger's hockey schools in some form.

In his endless quest to spread the good word about the game, Neilson operated his main camp, a not-for-profit enterprise, for the latter half of his life. He also ran a Christian hockey camp in Peterborough, and for several years, until the unrest in the Middle East grew too dangerous, he exported the game to a keen group of quick learners in Metulla, Israel. For sixteen years, Neilson brought together professional and amateur coaches at his annual coaches' clinic in Windsor, Ontario.

But it's the five-week residential camp that brings together forty years and more of Roger's relationships inside and outside the game. Two generations of families have come to work at Neilson's summer hockey school since the first one was established in Pembroke in 1970. After that, Roger was part of a Kawartha school in Peterborough for about five years and first established his

own program in Port Hope in the mid-1970s, when he stepped in to replace Howie Meeker.

He moved the camp to Lindsay in the mid-1990s.

For the five camp weeks, staff worked at a wild pace, taking just Saturdays as the day to let their hair down, or, in Roger's case, let it curl out from underneath his A&F cap.

Most, if not all, of the camp staff would land in for the day at Roger's house on Chemong Lake, east of Lindsay and northwest of Peterborough.

"Saturdays were crazy," says Darren Keily, a long-time camp staffer and one of Roger's important youth recruits. "We'd go tubing behind Roger's boat. We played road-hockey games. And the music would be blaring."

The standard Saturday-night meal was steak, potatoes, and corn, if Roger could get it. He loved a fresh cob of corn.

"We'd have a huge frying pan just full of mushrooms," says Keily. "It was the same meal every Saturday. He'd go out and buy dozens of steaks."

He bought so many steaks that Devin Smith of the NHL Players' Association, whose father, Ron, was an assistant coach with Roger, wonders how Roger's favourite local meat shop can survive after Neilson's passing.

Roger's great friend Colin Campbell tells a lovely story about Neilson and his camps. The NHL's senior vice-president and director of hockey operations, Campbell is best known as the NHL's chief judge and jury on player-discipline issues. But "Colie" was once a hard-nosed player from Tillsonburg, Ontario. He was drafted by Roger's OHL Peterborough Petes team in 1970 and also played for the Roger-coached Vancouver Canucks in the early 1980s.

In a tribute to Roger, Campbell told *The Hockey News* he was with his wife, Heather, driving their son, Gregory, to the first day of Roger's camp in Lindsay. It was about 7:00 in the morning, the grass still wet with dew, when Campbell saw this figure racing

across a field, posting direction signs for parents of campers. It was, of course, Roger Neilson.

"To me," said Campbell, "that was pure Roger."

It had all the elements. Neilson was a morning man and a man of detail. Holding one of his famous lists in his hand, Roger would meet with his camp staff early in the morning with directives on any number of issues, including schedules. He would then oversee the morning camp operation, perhaps sneak away for a bite or to read a book, and then maybe steal some rays behind the residence in the afternoon. (For a man who devoted himself to what he believed was the one true God, Neilson was an avid sun worshipper, a habit that likely shortened his life.)

When Roger was on the job, no element of camp life was too minor to escape his attention. That included a cup in the camp mini-putt course, a cup that runneth over, protruding a centimetre or two above the green. Nobody on earth took recreational pursuits more seriously than Roger Paul Neilson.

"It drove him crazy," says Larry Pearson, setting the scene of one of the better camp stories of 2002.

"He'd be thinking about it, thinking about it. Next thing we know, he's got a spoon in his hand. And here he is, down on his hands and knees, his tongue's hanging out, and he's digging away under this cup to get it down lower. Everything has to be perfect. There are no maybes.

"Here's a guy who hasn't been healthy for a few years, and he still sees that the cup's not right. The ground's rock hard. I think some of our rink rats had tried to fix it, but the ground was just too hard. And he finds a spoon. I think I have a picture of it. I thought, I have to get a shot of this. This is how meticulous he is.

"Roger could sometimes look as though he was distracted and not paying attention, but really, his ability to still focus on the little details and big picture was astounding – he knew what was coming down the tubes before anyone else did.

"You look at his coaching-clinic files, his hockey-school files, he'd have, on a piece of cardboard, a complete inventory list of what was present, down to every minute level, including hats, and key chains, this, this, this. Unbelievable logistics behind all this stuff. And he would see the big picture, like how much inventory we would have to have to get through this many closing ceremonies and deal with this many kids and whether we might have to source something out."

In many hockey camps, the headliner is a figurehead who makes brief appearances while a crew of lesser-knowns carries out the real work. Roger's camp was all Roger, his concepts, his plan, overseen by him every day. He didn't take days off. He walked the grounds, watched evening scrimmages. A ubiquitous presence.

More or less.

Kris King remembers his first impressions on joining "the band."

"Roger ran the show. He'd have a staff meeting the Sunday before, telling us all the rules, et cetera. The first time, I was real nervous. I mean, this was Roger Neilson, this was going to be unbelievable, and then I found out, everything he said, nobody listened to anyway. When he was around, it was like everyone was prim and proper and did their job, and when he kind of disappeared – he liked to go play golf or maybe fall asleep someplace – we'd just terrorize the place. He knew everything that was going on – he just chuckled."

Anyone who has worked in a Roger camp has seen, learned, memorized the marching orders as laid out in the staff manual. Detailed as it is, it doesn't begin to explain the camp hierarchy, from big chiefs to little rats.

Just below Neilson's role as director were the supervisors and managers like Bedford (camp director), Pearson, Clements, Bowen, Faulkner, and Starkman. Alex Andjelic, a European coach, and Kent Pearce were his chief on-ice instructors, alongside three recreational

instructors, several assistant on-ice instructors, two power-skating instructors, and more than a dozen camp counsellors. Finally, at the bottom of the hockey-operation totem pole are the "rats," short for rink rats. These young helpers are responsible for everything from fetching a meal for a hungry visitor like Eric Lindros (some of the pros get a lunch break and can personally visit the camp cafeteria) to cleaning dressing rooms, setting up equipment, and doing "puck searches" after all games and practices.

It's grunt work, but today's counsellors and instructors, nearly all of whom are rat graduates, say they loved being rats for one main reason: they got to spend more time with Roger than anyone else, because the rats were on the ground floor, carrying out his detailed master plan.

"It's totally changed now," says Kent Pearce, whose father, Tom, was a carrier on Roger's famed *Globe and Mail* route in Toronto. "We used to have a set schedule, like 10:05, go pick up pucks, 10:15, clean up this room and that room. It was pretty structured. There were only three of us back then, and now there's, like, eight of them. It was good, though. Back then, the rats were the ones who hung out with Roger the most, because Roger wanted to make sure all the little stuff was just perfect. So the rats did this and the rats did that. It was pretty good. My first year as a rat I was part of the group that went to Hawaii with him."

Of course, the rats might also feel the wrath if anything was askew. Signs had to be straight and erected at the right time. Loose garbage or a shortage of ping-pong balls was a capital offence in Roger's world.

Perhaps because games were so close to his heart, the games room was a constant source of irritation to him if things weren't in order.

"He'd walk in and say, 'The whole room up there's a mess,'" says Clements. "'It's filthy! What are the rats doing?'

"And you'd go up and there'd be three things on the floor."

Changing a minor detail of Roger's plan was akin to moving Whistler Mountain.

It took four years for the camp leaders to alter the structure so there were two, rather than three, award assemblies.

"It was fun arguing with him," says Clements. "He'd listen and get that look on his face, and he'd think about it, and then come back and say, 'Nah, I don't think so.' He'd let you think he was thinking about it, but he was a very stubborn man."

At 9:00, Sunday morning, the camp leaders and counsellors held their first staff meeting in preparation for the onslaught. The group held a moment's silence for Roger, then got on with business.

Within hours, more than a hundred smiling camper faces would be landing in, with their gear and their expectations, Roger or no Roger. Most of these kids would have been told that Neilson, the camp overseer and figurehead, had passed on. That didn't mean they expected to have anything less than a raging good time.

There were surprisingly few cancellations, despite Neilson's death and the SARS threat that had severely damaged the Ontario tourism industry in the summer of 2003. There was the one parent, however, who'd called to leave the sensitive message that she'd heard "*someone* had died and the camp wasn't going to be as good."

By week four, the realization was sinking in that Roger's Boys had pulled it off. Four weeks in the books without a major international incident. With or without Neilson, that was an accomplishment.

Of course, there were the usual crises. Misplaced underwear. Minor injuries. A teenaged camper swiped someone's cellphone and started calling sex-hotline numbers.

But by the time Eric Lindros of the New York Rangers arrived on the Friday of the fourth and penultimate week of camp, the

counsellors were starting to relax, like schoolteachers with all but the final days of June crossed out on their calendars.

The NHL players themselves may not realize it during their cameo appearances, but hockey camps go to great lengths to ensure that their star attractions are looked after. The bigger the star, the bigger the fuss.

In the case of Lindros, it means making arrangements to have him picked up by seaplane at his cottage on Lake Rosseau in the Muskokas. On the morning Lindros was to arrive at the Snug Harbour marina in Lindsay, the excitable camp directors sent not one, but two cars out to pick him up, concerned that the first driver might have missed him.

Lindros walked into the arena with his skates, gloves, and stick, picked up the envelope waiting for him in his stall, ripped it open, and handed the $500 honorarium cheque to me, mistaking me for one of the camp directors.

"Are the Muskies still operating?" asked Lindros.

"Uh, yeah," I replied, a little stunned to be holding Eric Lindros's paycheque in my hand.

"Well, give this to the Muskies."

It's a Lindros camp tradition, the annual bounced cheque. The camp hands him his fee, he bounces it right back to the operation.

In the Muskies dressing room, which serves as the hub for all counsellors and rink rats in between on-ice sessions, a bronze plaque recognizes the rejected fees of Lindros and Mike Ricci, which were used to buy television sets for the players.

One year, when Lindros told the camp to go buy a TV set for the junior team, he was reminded he'd already paid for one.

"Well, buy another one," he said.

No other hockey camp features as many NHL stars or retired pros, usually fifteen or more. A typical Neilson list might be Lindros, Ricci, Mike Fisher, Chris Neil, Kris King, Jody Hull, Doug

Jarvis, Jason Spezza, Ron Tugnutt, Mike Fountain, Dallas Eakins, Marc Crawford, Mike Murphy, Keith Acton, and Mike Hough.

Unlike the cameo pro appearances of some camps, Roger's NHLers always stay long enough to make an impact. In the wake of Roger's passing, the interaction with the kids is illuminating, uplifting. Comical Kris King, a former Maple Leaf and Ranger among his other stops, keeps the adults laughing even if some of his lines sail over the youngsters' heads like deflected slapshots.

"Hey, guys, how's everything at home?" King says to a group of boys as they approach the autograph table. "Your wives okay?"

To a wiry seven-year-old wearing a tank top, King says, "Wow, good cables. You work out?"

After all these years, camp organizers have the pro visits down to a science. Autograph sessions are held at a prescribed time. The campers line up like customers at a bank. For kids who don't have a hockey card or program to get signed, the pro can autograph from a stack of blank cards – blank other than the Roger Neilson signature stamp.

A boy of eight glances down at his freshly signed Lindros card and declares, "In ten years, this will be worth, like, a million dollars."

Lindros signs anything that isn't nailed down. Roger camp shirts. Sticks. Programs. Hats. A boy slides a Brett Lindros card in front of Eric. Right church. Wrong pew.

"Hey, that's all right," says Eric, signing his brother's card. "I just got three years younger."

Eric, who's been doing stints at Neilson camps since he was first coached by Roger in Philadelphia in 1998, says he can still feel the man's presence this first summer without him.

"His spirit," says Lindros, "is in every corner around here."

In the relative quiet of the Muskies dressing room, Lindros chows down on a chicken burger. "This is good," he says. "Can I get another one?" And one of the rink rats, suddenly with wings

on his feet, hustles back over to the campus cafeteria. It isn't every day a guy can run an errand for Number 88.

Lindros talks about his flight in from Muskoka, in a forty-year-old plane.

"My first question to the pilot is, 'So, how long you been flying?'

"He says, 'Since 1983.' So I'm thinking, that's okay.

"My second question is, 'Have you ever had any close calls?'

"And he says, 'Well, there was this one time . . .' and I'm like, okay, let's move on from here."

Lindros is talking easily now with me, sitting next to him in the dressing room and a roomful of rink rats and instructors pretending not to listen, chatting among themselves, but still straining to catch every word from his lips. Eric realizes that I'm a sportswriter, who once covered his junior games with the Oshawa Generals fourteen years ago, and am not one of the camp directors.

He looks me in the eye.

"Did I give you that cheque?"

Not that anyone would distrust a sportswriter, but Lindros is relieved to hear me say I'd turned the cheque over to the camp office.

Eric talks at length about Roger, his strengths as a coach and the value of his close relationship with him, which helped Lindros through his final, difficult months with the Flyers. Beyond his concussion issues, Lindros experienced other headaches from his dealings with Philadelphia management. Neilson was relief to Lindros. He was fresh air. In Philadelphia, Pennsylvania, or Lindsay, Ontario.

"I'd see Roger coming down from the gondola," says Lindros, "and he'd say, 'I'll be down in a minute.' And then he'd have to stop and talk to thirty people on the way down."

Now it's time to get to work, though Eric makes it feel like play. He walks into a dressing room filled with wide-eyed

teenagers, aged fourteen to sixteen, getting dressed for the camp semifinals. Throughout the week the scrimmages have been building to these "playoffs."

If the kids weren't motivated enough, here's Lindros in the room, giving them a chalk talk.

"Let's see if we can't open up the game a little bit," says Lindros, talk that might seem like sacrilege in the presence of the ghost of Roger Neilson, devout practitioner of defensive hockey.

Neilson used to joke about the extent of that reputation. "In Port Hope one summer," said Roger, "a father brought his son for a week and said he was glad to have him at my school because the kid 'didn't check very well.' "

Lindros sketches a simple breakout play.

"Get it out on the side where there's the least pressure," says Lindros.

Big Eric has already been on the ice, participating in one of the skills sessions. He's right into it, skating alongside the kids, chipping in with advice, and providing play-by-play: "Oh, what a save . . ."

"He's like a big kid out there," says Clements, looking on. "He'd much rather be on the ice than at the autograph table."

Professional hockey players get ripped if they leave a single person without an autograph, so it's reassuring to observe this other side – players going out of their way to provide kids with a special experience.

The highlight of the camp day is the semifinal scrimmage between the "Leafs" and "Canadiens." Eric goes behind the Leafs bench, helps direct his team to a 4-2 lead, then joins the Canadiens' bench halfway through.

The game ends 8-3, and the players on both sides have stories to tell their folks on the drive back home, if not to their grandchildren many years down the road.

Ink-Stained
and Devious

There was a time, apparently, when Roger Neilson was not a coach. It's almost disappointing to discover he didn't emerge from the womb barking at a game official or signalling for a hit-and-run play. Mind you, it's reassuring to know that few people remember the years when Roger *wasn't* coaching.

Neilson was coaching as a "hobby" by the time he was seventeen and attending university. The year was 1951. He couldn't have imagined that his coaching passion would be the ride of a lifetime, a ride that would take him all over the world.

Only in Roger's world could this possibly be considered a normal existence: coaching and working – delivering newspapers – in Toronto while commuting eighty kilometres to McMaster University in Hamilton five days a week. Not yet old enough to vote or decline his first drink, Neilson was already living his credo that a twenty-four-hour day was an opportunity for twenty hours

of activity. He was running the ultra-marathon years before the term was invented to describe long-distance maniacs.

Like most everything else in his life, the deep religious commitment of Roger and his family shaped the course of his future. With his sister, Joan, four years his senior, Roger grew up in north Toronto, in a charming house on Sheppard Avenue near Bayview. Today, Toronto's sprawl seems to begin at Lake Ontario and extend north to Newmarket and beyond, but in the 1940s and 1950s, farmland still dotted the growing suburbs to the east, west, and north. The Neilsons' backyard was a mini-farm of sorts, covering several acres and including a small apple orchard. A neighbour tended the orchard.

Norman Neilson, Roger's father, was an osteopath like his father, Robert James, before him. He manipulated patients' bones in the office-clinic he set up in the summer kitchen around the back of the house. Charis Neilson, Roger's mother, was born in Bulawayo, South Africa, and met her future husband in England after the First World War. Roger, who had nicknames for everyone, referred to his dad as "Whitey" for his grey hair.

The Neilsons led a simple life, unhampered by material goods. Norman Neilson did not own a car, nor did he care to accumulate wealth. Most of what he earned in his practice, Norman gave to the church, a habit not lost on his son. Among the family's few luxuries was an annual summer vacation to Haliburton. The Neilsons took a train north from Toronto and stayed in a rented cottage.

Charis Neilson was a strong-willed woman who would admonish Roger for his unkempt appearance (apparently to little effect). Friends of Roger's say that though his mother would try to lighten the tone of her instructions – "Do you think you could straighten your tie, Roger?" – she came across as rather serious.

Joan, extremely quiet and shy, grew up to be a church librarian and played the piano like an angel, whether in the church choir or family gatherings. Like Roger, she never married. Over the

years, she kept in touch with her little brother in letters and by telephone. Severely allergic to insect venom, Joan, as an adult, rarely visited Roger's summertime digs in Peterborough cottage country for fear of being stung by a bee. She carried with her a kit containing a vile of injectable epinephrine in the event of a sting, but generally reserved her visits to the Kawarthas to winter time.

Roger Neilson's family tree traces its Canadian roots back to the Scottish emigration of John Neilson from Paisley, Scotland, in 1821. John Neilson settled near the village of Almonte, west of Ottawa. The brother of Roger's grandfather – Roger's great-uncle, in other words – was the William Neilson who started the Neilson chocolate empire in 1893.

Roger was fond of saying he had "no living relatives," but it would seem this was not entirely true. While Neilson had no known first cousins, aunts, or uncles (neither of his parents had siblings), John Pellowe of Elmira, Ontario, has researched Neilson's genealogy and deduced that he had dozens of second cousins. Pellowe himself is a third cousin. "He has lots of relatives," says Pellowe, executive director of the Canadian Council of Christian Charities.

Roger's family attended the nearby People's Church on Sheppard Avenue and held Gideon Bible Society meetings in their home. The boys on Neilson's baseball teams in the 1950s say Roger didn't talk about religion as a young coach. If they were on a road trip or at a tournament, Neilson would simply take his players to church on Sunday.

"We knew religion was a big part of his life," says Doug Peacock, who played hockey for Roger on his Ted Reeve and Leaside teams. "We knew he went to the People's Church and we found that interesting because it was different."

If the span between birth and coaching debut was brief, Roger's pre-newspaper days were practically the blink of an eye. From age nine, Roger delivered the *Globe and Mail* newspaper. The route, which he held for twenty-three years, developed into a cottage industry, laced with romantic tales and apocryphal anecdotes.

In Roger's later years, as the tributes poured in and his legend became widespread, the *Globe* route became a fishing story, and the fish grew larger with each telling. Depending on who provided the account, the tale got to be so tall that only Paul Bunyan, never mind Roger Paul Neilson, could have delivered the one thousand or two thousand or ten thousand newspapers in the yarn.

There wasn't much need to stretch the newspaper story, although Neilson himself may have nudged it along. The truth was formidable enough. According to Pearce and other Roger helpers on the route, the total number of customers didn't exceed 800 to 850 at any time. Brian Bell was a key delivery boy in the mid-1960s and recalls a typical Roger route of 400 to 450 papers. In the 1950s, it was smaller.

"It was a good business," said Neilson. "I started when I was nine and it just kept getting bigger and bigger. It cost customers five cents a copy when I started. The *Star* was three cents. And when the *Globe* went to seven cents, there was an awful outcry. Thirty-five cents a week and people went crazy."

Usually, Neilson did the route with a couple of helpers, at one time including future hockey coach Dick Todd, whom Neilson nurtured in sport until Todd saw his name engraved on the Stanley Cup with the 1994 New York Rangers as an assistant coach.

Neilson was attached to the paper route for obvious reasons. It paid his way through university, a degree in education at McMaster. If being an average student meant working a little, partying a little, and sleeping a lot, then Roger was hardly an average student. At age seventeen, he was coaching peewee

hockey in Toronto, attending university classes in Hamilton, and delivering several hundred newspapers each morning.

"With a schedule like that, we all had bets Roger would not see the age of thirty-five," says Terry "Mo" O'Malley, a long-time member of Canada's national hockey team and now president of Notre Dame College in Saskatchewan.

The O'Malleys and the Drapers – Mike is the father of Chris Draper of the Detroit Red Wings and Dave is a pro scout – also delivered the *Globe* in north Toronto.

"Each summer in August, on Saturdays, we'd rent the ice at Toronto's Leaside arena at 4:00 a.m. before we did our paper routes," says O'Malley. "It was shinny time, and Roger was the leader who organized everything. We'd have to help Roger with his papers afterwards, because we wouldn't get started until about 6:00 a.m."

When he started teaching in Toronto, Neilson was paid six dollars an hour. He could do better than that tossing *Globe*s onto porches. Christmas tips alone got to be worth $2,000 to $2,500 per season. (Roger made sure each customer received a Christmas card with his name on it, just to encourage positive payback.) He made about $5,000 a year in regular earnings.

The 5:00 a.m. start to his work day became a lifelong habit.

"We lived on Heathview, a few blocks away," says Bell. "He'd come by at 5:00, and if I wasn't awake he'd walk around the side of the house and rap on my bedroom window.

"We got our papers at Yonge and St. Clair. There were usually three of us and Roger's dog, Jacques. There was a donut shop we always stopped at and they'd give Jacques a plain donut."

The first section of the route mostly comprised a series of apartment complexes – warm escapes for the wintertime carrier – near Yonge and St. Clair. Then the group drove through Old Forest Hill Road to Eglinton and scooped a second bundle of papers. That took the Roger Express into the classy environs of Forest Hill Village.

These were the good old days of newspaper delivery, when rolling up a paper was a work of art, folding it perfectly to withstand a throw from the sidewalk or curb.

"One person would roll papers in the van and another would run alongside, with maybe fifty, sixty papers in a sack," says Bell. "And he'd meet Roger at the corner."

The business brought a lifetime of pride to Roger. Long after he'd moved away and become a full-time hockey coach, he would occasionally return to Toronto with an important companion, such as Nancy Nichols, and retrace the route, providing a shadow demonstration of his style with a rolled-up newspaper flying out of a moving truck.

"He could hit the open door of this one house," says Bell. The customer wanted the paper *inside* the house and, spring through fall, left the front door wide open. "Of course, it wasn't enough just to hit it. The challenge every morning for Rog was to drive by as quickly as he could. Rog would start biting his tongue getting ready. He could roll a paper like nobody else – it would never fall apart – and he would flip that left-side door of the van open and throw with his left hand, driving purposely as fast as he could.

"It was a challenge to see how fast he could drive and still put it through the door and into the vestibule of this place. I don't think I ever saw him miss."

Neilson said there was another house that wanted it thrown into a second-storey window so the customer could read it in bed. He said he took great pride in hitting the target five times out of six.

As any carrier can attest, "collecting" was often the worst part of the job. Direct payment was a blessing, but for the rest of the weekly accounts, Neilson and his crew would go door to door. He would sometimes recruit his peewee hockey or baseball teams, giving them a 10-per-cent cut of their returns, to fan out and sweep the neighbourhood.

Ruby Bell, Brian's mother, was most impressed at the way Roger encouraged his paper-route helpers to open bank accounts and deposit a portion of their earnings. "It was their first experience at earning money," she said, "and saving money."

Roger, rounding into form as a mentor, used to say a paper route was "the best thing for a kid. It teaches discipline. You might be sick and have to miss school, but you can't miss delivering the papers. There can be wicked snowstorms, but you still have to do it. I only missed when I had to go out of town with the hockey team."

When Neilson was hired by Sam Pollock and Scotty Bowman to run the Peterborough Petes, the OHA junior farm team of Pollock's Montreal Canadiens, Neilson handed the route over to Dick Todd but asked him to hang on to it, "just in case it doesn't work out in Peterborough."

In his spare time, such as it was, Roger was a decent athlete, definitely not one of the "those who can't, teach" types. He was about five-foot-nine, with a sturdy frame. It would be years before Neilson would let out those famous curly locks; early Rog favoured a severe crewcut that gave him the look of a marine recruit on those rare occasions he appeared without a ball cap on his head.

Roger learned sport from the ground up before he was hitting fungoes and charting the neutral-zone trap. But how quickly he evolved from one to the other. And that's where his religious background came into the picture. As an evangelical Christian, Norman Neilson strictly forbade Roger from participating in Sunday sport. If that sounds harsh and archaic, keep in mind that in the late 1940s and early 1950s, the senior Neilson had plenty of support for keeping Sunday holy by resting rather than playing games. The city of Ottawa, for example, lost its Triple-A baseball team in 1954

largely because of Mayor Charlotte Whitton's successful referendum in favour of banning Sunday baseball at Lansdowne Park. Decades earlier, Lord Stanley's own sons were once chastised by a church pastor for being among those youth who "joined in the game and gloried in its shame."

Roger came to adopt his father's stance on sport-free Sundays, only giving up when he settled into coaching at the major junior level.

Ironically, this imposed day of rest helped shape him as a sportsman. Driven by boredom, Roger would spend entire Sunday afternoons playing backyard games of his own invention – the equivalent of an artist doodling. He played, he schemed, and he dreamed, all the while falling in love with sport, to his parents' surprise if not dismay.

Although he would later get mileage out of mocking his own athletic abilities, Roger was a pretty good Junior B goaltender for the Woodbridge Dodgers, northwest of Toronto. Doug Peacock, who played on some of the earliest minor-hockey teams coached by Roger, says that Neilson had been a part of the renowned Toronto Marlboroughs chain but wasn't allowed to play for the Marlies' Weston Dukes because he refrained from playing Sunday games.

"Roger wouldn't speak ill of anyone, but I think he felt he was mistreated by Stafford Smythe and the Marlies organization, and that motivated him," says Peacock. "It was a big thing to him, trying to beat the Marlies. He wanted to put together a team to compete with the Marlies and he did that by building the Leaside Rangers organization, which became affiliated with the New York Rangers."

Roger started the process of chasing the Marlies by coaching peewee kids cut by the Marlies. It wouldn't be the last time he would dabble in the business of coaching spurned, and highly motivated, players.

One of Neilson's friendly early rivals was Harry Neale, now a *Hockey Night in Canada* broadcaster.

"Roger grew up in the next school district over from me," says Neale. "He went to North Toronto Collegiate; I went to Lawrence Park. He was a couple of years older than me, but in our travels, whether it was playing baseball at Eglinton Park or THL [Toronto Hockey League] hockey, our paths would cross.

"He had a group of guys that played road hockey. Two or three Saturdays every spring, his street would play my street on a neutral site, a public school. We were twelve, thirteen, fourteen, then he went on to play for Woodbridge. His last year was my first with the Weston Dukes, so I played against him."

Neale remembers Neilson as a decent goaltender and a candidate to move up to major junior.

"Hap Emms was coaching the Barrie Flyers at the time, and he wanted Roger to come up to Barrie for a tryout. But Roger's mom and dad were very religious and didn't want him going where he'd have to play on a Sunday. He was a pretty good Junior B goalie, so I could see why a Junior A team would be interested in him.

"I don't know whether that stopped him from pursuing a career in hockey, but Roger was a very religious guy, so I wouldn't be surprised."

Roger's self-deprecating response to that compliment was that he more or less played to his level.

Once he made the decision to turn his attention to coaching, Neilson swept onto the sandlot scene with the force of a high-grade hurricane.

At age seventeen, he was behind the bench directing a group of youngsters on a sponsored hockey team called Dave's White Rose. The next season he coached a bantam B hockey team called Ideal Welding, the perfect sponsor to represent Neilson's philosophy of a club bonding together to do great things. And it did – Ideal

Welding provided Roger with his first minor-hockey championship.

When he was twenty-four, he had his first city-league championship team on the ball field, the Sasco Tubes.

Neilson got a kick out of the wacky and varied sponsors he cajoled into supporting his boys of summer and winter. In fact, he was proud to have done his part to put the Bick's Pickles company on the map.

"I had a major-midget team in the years when [the THL] was a really good league," said Roger. "If you beat the Toronto Marlies one year out of six, you had really accomplished something. This was way back before Bick's Pickles were well known. But Mr. Bick gave us some money, and he said, 'You gotta call the team Bick's Pickles.' I had [future Leaf] Brian Glennie on that team. The uniform had a big pickle on the front. That's how his business got started.

"Then there was Dave's White Rose – that was a peewee team. Dave gave us $250, and so we were Dave's White Rose. I had 'em all. I had the Day Sign Company, and it wasn't Hap Day, either.

"When I was going to McMaster University I was coaching three teams, hockey and baseball," Neilson told the *Globe and Mail*. "During the summer I'd get a job with the parks and recreation department [in Toronto] and organize games with the kids."

Here's where the overlap paid off. Neilson was a little worried one summer that his parks-and-rec job could be in jeopardy if not enough kids signed up for the summer activity days. No problem. Roger just rounded up his ballplayers and brought them out for the rec-department games. Instant enrolment, nudged along by the master recruiter.

Though he would make his name in hockey, Neilson loved the influence he could have in a ball game. In hockey, he used to say, once a coach prepares his team and sorts out his lines, he more or less helplessly sends his players over the boards to succeed or fail.

In baseball, though, Roger could feel the grit of the diamond in his teeth. He could smell the lime of the basepaths, which he occasionally set himself. He relished the idea of communicating to each of his batters with a signal from the third-base coaching box. He could call for a steal, a hit-and-run, or, in the case of the apple trick, hide it, throw it, eat it, or bury it. Roger Ball was a lot like Billy Ball, the tag given to the aggressive managing style of Billy Martin in the 1970s and 1980s.

It was "little ball" micromanaging, designed to put pressure on the less-than-perfect defensive abilities of the average eleven, twelve, and thirteen-year-old ballplayer. Roger was merciless in exploiting weaknesses, putting the onus on Little League opponents to make perfect throws. He liked his chances in that kind of game. "We did a lot of double steals, got in rundowns to score a guy from third," said Larry Oakley, who played for one of Roger's Peterborough teams. "We manufactured runs – if we got five or six hits, we'd score five runs."

As he would with his hockey teams, Neilson introduced gimmicks and bribes to mask the boredom of repeating fundamentals at practice. He would put up twenty-five-cents to the player who could lay down the most consecutive bunts on ten pitches. Dick Todd remembers concentrating with all his will to earn that quarter.

Writer Jay Teitel was another of Roger's charges in Toronto. In a story for *Toronto Life* magazine, Teitel described Neilson's practices in terms of poetic rapture.

It was heady, professional sport to me: the equipment, the big league order everywhere. First we ran bases to a stopwatch. Then, we learned how to slide, regular slide and hook slide, both sides of the bag. Up to this point Roger had mainly directed and watched. But now he threw batting practice and I can only say that it was joyous. He threw the way he drove, rhythmic, efficient, ancient, holding seven balls at a time in an

old borrowed glove, never really stopping his motion, cranking up and throwing, waiting for the crack of the bat, not turning to follow the ball, but starting his studied wind-up again. And the pitches, they came in waist high and perfect, hard enough to test you but not so hard that they would overpower you. I hit one, then another and then I found myself praying that the dream would not end.

It's easy to love a sport when a skipper is as consistently successful as Neilson. Baseball championships littered his curriculum vitae. He especially thrilled to the underdog role, upsetting the favourite. And that wasn't an easy trick in his other sport.

"Coaching minor hockey in that era, you went against the Marlboroughs," said Neilson. "We won once in hockey. Any team had a chance in baseball." Evidently, Roger's teams had the best chance. He coached nine championship ball teams in ten years.

Dave Clements quipped to *Toronto Sun* baseball writer Bob Elliott, "When it comes to Roger's likes, hockey would be third, behind coaching baseball and delivering the *Globe and Mail.*"

Before Neilson, the Little League baseball association in his home district of North Toronto was "at its lowest point," according to an item in the *Toronto Star* in the summer of 1959. Credited for the rebirth was none other than a certain twenty-five-year-old schoolteacher with the initials R.N., which sometimes stood for Register, Now!

Neilson had his finger in all sorts of pies. He became president of the North Toronto league and was also coaching three teams in three different age groups. Ah, the good old days before conflicts of interest. Neilson was the happy executive with the diamond dirt between his toes.

"About one month ago," the *Star* reported, "Neilson bought a small bus to transport his players around the city for exhibition

games and to Eglinton Park, where the league operates every week-night and Saturday morning."

And, of course, never on Sunday. "He had to go through hoops to stop our games from being scheduled on Sunday," says Todd, who pitched baseball for Roger and eventually coached junior hockey alongside him.

"When he is not coaching," the news story continued, "Neilson is president and co-ordinator of operations. . . . Neilson, in the hockey season, is area supervisor for the New York Rangers, who have five farm teams operating at Leaside Arena."

For a religious young man, Roger the coach was at least as devious as he was devout. If Neilson were a modern-day coach in minor hockey or baseball, he would undoubtedly be called on the carpet of minor-league administrators to explain his tactics and questionable sportsmanship. He would be chastised by rival parents and coaches, perhaps even drummed out of sport. To his distinct advantage, Roger coached amateur sport at a time when parents stayed home and kept their noses out of the world of a coach and his kids.

To tell tales of Roger Neilson is to look back at a distant, presumably more innocent time, and because the tales involve Roger, his hijinks – at the ballpark and in the arenas from atom hockey to junior – draw howls of laughter when the stories are told. But picture yourself as the parent of an opposing pitcher when Roger was encouraging his team to razz him, taunt him, and use whatever other means to throw him off his game. Neilson's gang went far beyond the chant of "pitcher's got a rubber arm."

"We were awful," says Clements, who played for Roger in the second phase of Neilson's baseball coaching career, the Peterborough era from 1970 to 1975. "We were a really aggravating bunch. We'd be chirping their pitcher, chirping everybody. And he encouraged it. You couldn't do that today."

Once, when his team was up against a particularly tough pitcher, he urged his batters go up to the plate backwards, that is,

right-handed if they normally batted left and left-handed if they were righties. They were instructed to dance in the box, drop the barrel of the bat into a bunting position, all while the pitcher was still in his windup. The result was a rattled pitcher, a slew of walks, and a Neilson team victory.

Roger would become famous for testing and exploiting rules of hockey in major junior and the NHL, but it was on the sandlots that Neilson perfected the art. Catching an opposition coach napping, Roger would send up his top four batters over and over, bypassing the rest of the order, at a time when teams didn't always keep track of the opposition's batting lineup. Roger strikes – and wins – again.

Later Neilson would say, "Kids need a good caper once in a while."

Of course, the most famous Neilson baseball prank of all was the ol' hidden-apple trick. With an enemy runner on third base, Neilson would have his catcher throw what appeared to be a base-ball wildly over the third baseman's head. The runner would trot home, thinking he's scoring easily, only to discover the real ball was still in the catcher's mitt. Meanwhile, the left fielder would dispose of the biodegradable evidence by stomping on it.

Rob Campbell, one of Roger's early players, remembers one time when a particularly nervous umpire was forced to deal with the hidden ball–apple diversion. "Yerrr safe . . .," he called as the run scooted in, but then, in amendment, "uh, YERRRRRR OUT!"

Years later, Roger's Peterborough-area teams, well versed in the lore, used to beg their coach to let them try the apple trick. Trouble was, the tale had already made the rounds of sandlot gath-erings throughout the province. Roger's boys weren't the only ones up on the scheme. Clements, who caught for Roger on the Keene Expos, remembers the time they huddled on the mound and Roger deftly slipped him the apple to set the play in motion.

"The guy on third base was [former NHL star] Doug Gilmour's brother, Dave," says Clements. "I threw it over his head and he

Roger, age one. When his tongue emerged, he meant business. *(Courtesy Roger Neilson estate)*

Roger, at four, already set for the seas. Sister Joan was seven. *(Courtesy Roger Neilson estate)*

Early portrait: a rare shot of Roger sitting still. *(Courtesy Roger Neilson estate)*

Roger's bantam rugby football team won the 1948 Toronto Secondary Schools Athletic Association championship. He's front row, far left, No. 23. Author of a 23-skidoo play? *(Courtesy Roger Neilson estate)*

Roger, sans mask, backed the 1952-53 Weston Dukes to a championship season while coaching a bantam team to a city title. *(Courtesy Roger Neilson estate)*

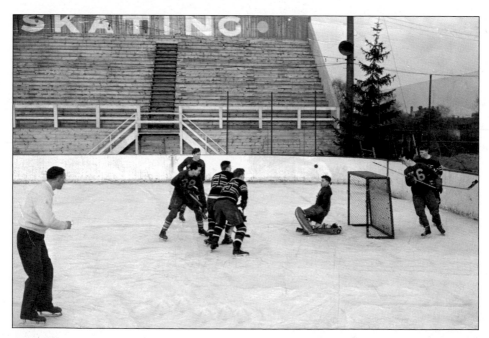

Roger in action. He may have learned this dropped-leg style from too many road hockey games. *(Courtesy Roger Neilson estate)*

Roger with the 1954-55 Shopsy's Pee Wees. *(Hockey Hall of Fame)*

Jacques, Roger's first "great" dog, worked his way into a few team photos. Here he's with the 1966 Richardson's Richardson's midgets team. *(Courtesy Roger Neilson estate*

Ken Dryden, future goaltending star, hockey executive, and member of parliament, was an early rival of Roger's ball teams. Dryden, at right, pitched for Kingsway. *(Courtesy Roger Neilson estate)*

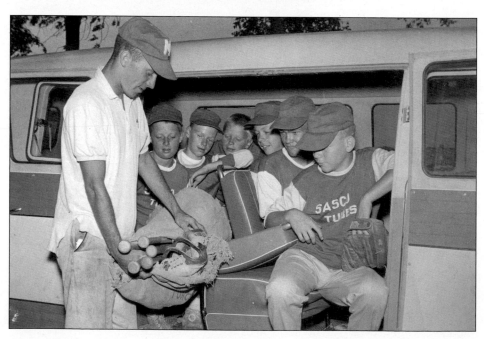

Roger's Volkswagen van helped the twenty-four-year-old deliver newspapers, equipment, players, and dogs. *(Toronto Star)*

If the man in the referee's outfit looks familiar, he should. Hall-of-Famer Maurice "Rocket" Richard stands in with Roger's Bick's Pickles midget club. *(Courtesy Roger Neilson estate)*

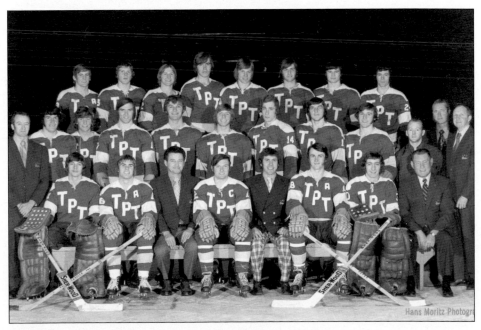

Neilson, front row in plaid pants, and his Peterborough Petes. On or off ice, he loved his checks. *(Hockey Hall of Fame)*

Not surprisingly, Roger lost the wedding band when he was best man for Dick Todd, right, but found it in time for the ceremony. *(Courtesy Roger Neilson estate)*

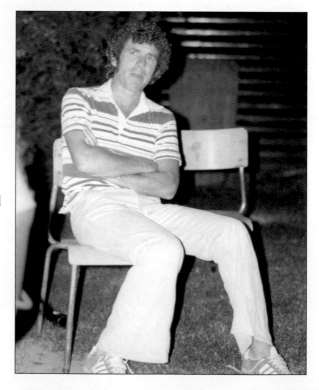

The *Globe and Mail* once described Neilson's physical appearance as "a cross between Elliott Gould and Robin Phillips." *(Courtesy Roger Neilson estate)*

Roger's NHL debut as head coach of the 1977-78 Toronto Maple Leafs was an occasion. Pierre Elliott Trudeau agreed. *(Courtesy Roger Neilson estate)*

Towel Power: Roger's spontaneous act of surrender with the Vancouver Canucks in 1982 introduced the sea of white to the game of hockey. *(Bruno Torres)*

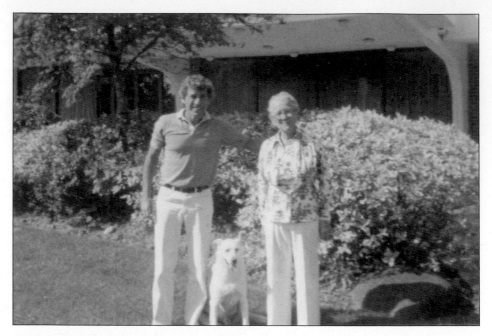

With two of his loved ones: his mother and Mike. *(Courtesy Roger Neilson estate)*

Todd Ervin was like a son to Roger. After Todd died in 1985, Roger held a Todd Reunion Week, inviting all of Todd's friends from Vancouver to Ontario for a series of activities in the boy's honour.
(Courtesy Ervin family)

just stood there laughing. I think he might have played for Roger, or he at least knew about it. By then the play was famous. Somebody even yelled, 'Hidden-ball play.'"

Weekend Magazine, in a piece on Roger Neilson in April 1975, referred to this as "the Bugs Bunny side of a non-drinking, non-smoking member of the evangelical People's Church . . . the side that has unnerved opposing coaches so much that they now believe any unnatural happening during a game is another Neilson caper."

Example: In an OHA semifinal series pitting Neilson's Peterborough Petes against the Kitchener Rangers in 1974, the power went out during the third period. Neilson denied having anything to do with it, but he readily admitted to a previous sin of this nature. That was during a ball game in Toronto in 1970. When the lights came back on, the opposition pitcher looked at home plate to face a bloodied mannequin hanging from the backstop. The prank was designed to unnerve him: he had discovered a dead body in a ravine a few weeks earlier.

Unfortunately for Neilson, the ploy failed. The body finder had nerves of steel. Guess the real corpse had toughened him.

Oh well, Roger no doubt mumbled to himself. It was worth a shot.

Neilson had as many tricks as he had players willing to carry them out.

Even the warm-up presented an opportunity to scheme. Campbell remembers how Roger's team would have a game scheduled for 7:00 in the evening at Talbot Park, one of the classier fields in the city. But his players would meet and warm up several blocks away at Eglinton Park. Just before 7:00, with the other team already imagining a no-show and a forfeit, Rog and his boys would show up in a blaze of glory, piling out of his van all loose and primed like Notre Dame football players jumping out of the Trojan Horse against the University of Southern California.

From the beginning, Roger was looking for the tiniest edge. And the man who would become known for craving grinding, working-class players in his NHL lineups exhibited the same taste for muckers when he was coaching runny-nosed kids.

"There was a shortstop on one peewee team named Billy Low, who looked just a like a beagle," Rob Campbell told the *Toronto Sun*. "Roger took such pleasure in working with him. But Roger was really competitive and anyone he knows would endorse that. He relished the underdog role and enjoyed thumbing his nose at teams that were more well off than his."

In baseball, as with hockey, Roger's pranks and rule manipulation often obscured his coaching excellence and attention to detail. Neilson was a stickler about practice regimen and thought nothing of throwing 200 pitches in batting-practice sessions. His players say he threw with such accuracy, 200 pitches meant 200 strikes.

As a schoolteacher and amateur coach, Roger created his little Toronto empire, then had to build one all over again in Peterborough, when Montreal Canadiens general manager Sam Pollock hired Neilson to coach the Petes.

A thirty-two-year-old bachelor moving to a new city might have felt he had his hands full with a major junior hockey team and a full-time teaching job at a local high school. But consider that Neilson had built up sixteen years of frenetic multi-tasking to this point.

Besides, it was bad enough that Roger had to give up his paper route; there was no way he was going to stop coaching baseball.

After taking a couple of years to settle into the job as coach and general manager of the Petes, Roger assessed the amateur landscape heading into the 1970 season. Baseball was already well

established in Peterborough. Teams were set. He didn't see an entry point, so he expanded his viewfinder and looked to the surrounding area. He was a man on a mission.

Southeast of the city on County Road 34 toward Rice Lake he stumbled upon the village of Keene. It once had some organized baseball, so at least had a diamond. It was a start.

Roger held tryouts, recruiting children from the local church, then the local school. He scoured the countryside for potential players in little burgs like Warsaw, Lakefield, Norwood, Donwood, Keene, towns that were seventy or eighty kilometres apart in some cases, east, south, and north of Peterborough.

Dave Clements was a typical recruit. Lean and blessed with speed, he was training for the 100-metre sprint one afternoon at Crestwood Secondary. Roger's school.

"You wonder how the universe aligns itself in a certain way," says Clements. "I'm running down the track, minding my own business, and suddenly Rog comes over and says, 'You want to play ball?'"

Neilson quickly nicknamed Clements "Appaloosa," in honour of the horse breed, for his quick feet. It was later shortened to "Ap." And Ap the sprinter would eventually run a lifelong marathon with Roger and his causes.

"It's like becoming one of Jesus' disciples," Clements says.

Trouble was, these apostles couldn't hit a fastball. Not yet.

Roger's Toronto experience served him well. He kept a supply of bats and balls, supplemented what he needed at local sporting goods stores and scrounged up uniforms that his eager country charges wished could have come with operating instructions. Why are there two pairs of socks? they wanted to know.

In their white uniforms with green and black trim, an Expos logo on the cap, the Keene Expos were born.

In no way did the logistical challenge of geography alter Roger's stubborn practice tradition, even if it meant an eighty-kilometre run

to round up his new heroes. Neilson had travelled that distance daily, remember, to attend university.

"He would start in Ennismore," says Larry Pearson, one of Roger's Donwood recruits. "Then he'd go down through Lakefield, Warsaw, and so on, every night. We'd stop for ice cream on the way home, then he'd drop everybody off. This was the routine."

Roger heard that a kid named John Kemp, a year older than the rest of Roger's midget-age players, could really throw a ball. Kemp was down watching the kids one day, and Roger invited him to join the next practice. Kemp stepped on the rubber and threw a couple of bullets to the catcher.

"That's it," said Roger, "we're moving up to juvenile. We're not midgets any more."

Neilson signed Kemp, and the kids were off to juvenile class, some of them playing over their heads in more ways than one.

Remarkably, the team's own shortcomings, such as their home-sweet-home field, sometimes worked in their favour.

"The Brockville Bunnies would show up," says Pearson. "They played against teams in the States, looked like a million dollars, had six pitchers warming up, and tons of equipment and multi-coaches, but what threw them off was the fact we had no mound."

Paul Bedford remembers when a team from the posh Toronto suburb of Don Mills arrived in Keene. "There was no mound and the infield was like cement," he says. "They refused to play us, the field was so bad."

Gradually, Roger's bad news bears rounded into a ball team. And as Hollywood would have it, the end was fitting. In what may have been one of Roger's best, if little known, coaching feats, the ragtag rookie outfit proceeded to win the juvenile D championship in their first year.

Roger got trophies for his champions. And the village of Keene held a parade down the main street with the ballplayers

riding on the community fire truck. "They tried to make it a big parade," said Roger, "but there were only a hundred people in the whole town."

Years later, when he was coaching in the NHL, Neilson would say, "It's funny, but when you get right down to it, it hasn't changed at all. It's the same business. You want to win really bad. You try everything you can to win. You hope that your team is motivated to win. But if it does, there's no difference. I'm not usually an emotional person, but the happiest I've ever been in my life was when the Keene Expos beat the Kendall Eagles for the juvenile D baseball championship. I threw my scoreboard over the backstop."

Instead of being content to rule juvenile D, Roger quickly raised the bar for his Keene-ers. "What's the point of winning D again?" he said.

And so the plucky Expos moved into the Triple-A loop, beating out teams from Brockville and Don Mills before losing to Hamilton in the finals.

The Expos became local legends. To this day, a member of the team can be at a Peterborough area ballpark, arena, or shopping mall and have some elderly person come up to him and say, "I used to watch you play for the Keene Expos!"

"The community got behind us," says Bedford. "Rog would organize a community dance to pay for uniforms. He would advertise. We got two hundred or three hundred fans out by the end. Roger had the name, and the team was winning. People started coming out. It was kind of a phenomenon for a while.

"But I mean it was all Rog. His coaching. We didn't have a friggin' clue."

So rich are the stories of Roger's coaching exploits, it's easy to forget he was a full-time schoolteacher in Toronto and Peterborough from the mid-1950s until 1973.

Teacher Roger focused on physical education, a natural home for the coach, but he also taught some history and English. Brian Bell was a student of Roger's in a rare science class at Bayview Junior High in Toronto. "It definitely wasn't Roger's thing," he says.

But connecting with youth was, and always would be, Roger's thing.

"He was out to help people he felt were going astray," remembers Bell. "We became friends because he saw me standing out in the hallway one time in grade eight and knew I was in trouble for something."

An adult who pays heed to a youth in trouble without snitching to his parents, quickly gains trust, and at the newly built Bayview Junior High in the late 1950s until 1966, Neilson related to students as though he were one himself, understanding the challenges and frustrations. Roger helped turn fellow instructors into "student's teachers," in the way that Roger was always a "player's coach." Bell says it was a remarkable experience to be among a group of teachers that connected with students on their level. "It was like they eliminated a generational difference in his presence."

Doug Peacock, who played hockey for Roger in the late 1950s and early 1960s, remembers players flocking to Roger. Peacock became an educator, like Neilson, and eventually principal of Crestwood Secondary School in Peterborough, where Roger taught in the 1970s. Now retired, Peacock writes a weekly column for the *Examiner* and penned this about Neilson:

Young people are always unconsciously searching for role models. They look for someone who likes them, listens to them, and is somewhat like them. They want to believe in people who will stand up for them and who are at ease in their company. It's not easy for adults to demonstrate these traits to youth. Roger found it easy . . . he remembered what it's like to be 16.

Tom Pearce, one of Roger's first students at Bayview, remembers Roger as a "bit of a rebel."

"He wouldn't wear a tie. He said he had an excuse, that he taught phys. ed. He wore what we'd call today a golf shirt and slacks."

Dave Clements was in Neilson's grade-eleven phys. ed. class in Peterborough. He recalls Neilson as an instructor who "went against the grain."

"In those days, you'd have maybe ten days to teach a unit, let's say volleyball or basketball," says Clements, one of many Roger disciples to become teachers in his likeness. "You were supposed to teach skills for eight days, then maybe the last couple of days throw in a couple of scrimmages, just to give the kids a bit of fun. For him, that was almost backwards. He'd want a couple of days of skills and have seven, eight days of games, because he knew that ultimately kids loved having games. So his idea was to make phys. ed. as much fun as possible. And he loved little tournaments. Everything for him is like a little tournament. Everything's competitive, yet keep it on the light side, where you're not ready to kill each other to win."

While the curriculum was designed to discourage competition in the gym, Neilson fostered competition. Similarly, his hockey school philosophy was to combine one hour of fun competition with every hour of skills.

In Peterborough, Neilson was the head coach of the biggest team in town, the major junior Petes. That meant he was a Big Man on Campus at Crestwood Secondary School, except that he hardly flaunted his status as a hockey coach and teacher.

Bedford remembers it was nearly Christmas of his first year in Neilson's class when he went to a Petes game with a friend. Bedford saw Roger walk across the ice to the players' bench and said, "That looks like my phys. ed. teacher!" Bedford's pal said, "You donkey, of course it is. It's Roger Neilson."

Neilson was a good teacher, according to Bedford, although he was not a great marker. "A set of tests would be on the table and the garbage can would be [right next to it], and each week they'd get a bit closer to the edge. Sometimes you'd get tests back in two months, sometimes you didn't get them back."

Bedford claims that as soon as the curriculum called for Roger to read books, he went to the Petes and asked to be made a full-time general manager and head coach.

Neilson planted roots in the Kawarthas that would last his lifetime. Early in his Crestwood days, Roger rented a cottage on Katchawanooka Lake, near Lakefield. Fellow teacher Mac Brick, whose home was on Chemong Lake, used to ride with Roger on a bus to school.

"One day," says Brick, "Roger asked me, 'Do you know of any places for sale near you?'

" 'Sure, why?'

" 'Because mine burned down yesterday.' "

Neilson lost all of his worldly possessions – most notably his hockey memorabilia – in that 1969 fire, caused when an oil stove ignited after Roger left for school. He soon bought a house – a fixer-upper – on Buckhorn Lake and remained there until 1985, when he moved to Chemong, his permanent residence thereafter.

Roger Neilson got his first nibble from professional hockey in the mid-1960s, when Scotty Bowman, then a scout for the Montreal Canadiens, asked him to be a regional scout in Toronto. Roger didn't have any illusions about the reason behind the offer. "I had a good midget team and the Canadiens wanted my players [for the Habs farm team in Peterborough]. To get my players, they made me a scout."

General manager Sam Pollock, the genius behind Montreal's dynasties of the 1960s and 1970s, was impressed with Neilson's ability to get the most out of his players. It wouldn't escape the notice of the shrewd Pollock that Neilson was competing against the powerful Toronto Marlies, and sometimes winning, with teams that were essentially Marlie castoffs. Pollock hired Neilson to work with the Petes in the fall of 1966 in an entry position involving player personnel. A month later, Roger would have a new job description. It was an omen. These circumstances would roughly repeat themselves about fifteen years later in Vancouver, with the Canucks. A coach gets suspended. Neilson shines in relief.

In both cases, an old-time brawl played a part.

No wonder Neilson wasn't opposed to fighting in hockey. It kept doing wonders for his career. In December 1966, an off-ice fight launched him as a coach at the major junior level.

During a game between the Oshawa Generals and a Petes team coached by Roger Bedard, the opposing coaches began arguing and, eventually, trading punches. Both were suspended for six games.

Neilson was chosen as a temporary replacement over Montreal Canadiens scout Claude Ruel and a couple of other candidates, in part because it was the school Christmas break and Roger the teacher was ready and available.

He didn't wait to put his stamp on major junior hockey. In his first game behind the bench, Roger made roster moves, line changes, and switched his goalies, Randy Reid and Gary Holbrook, every five minutes just to get his opponents, the London Nationals, wondering what on earth was going on. Neilson lost only once in his six-game stint. Bedard returned behind the bench after his suspension but soon resigned his position, and Neilson took over full time.

This would be a ten-year stay. In seven of the ten years, Neilson taught at Crestwood and hustled over to the Peterborough Memorial Centre after school. By 1973, he was a full-time coach and GM, earning a handsome thirty grand and able to drop his

teaching gig. For that compensation, he was also expected to be the club's chief scout, publicity director, and receptionist.

Though he wouldn't be hung with the "Captain Video" label until he coached in Toronto, it was in Peterborough that Neilson first used video for hockey instruction.

"I was teaching high school, and we used audio-video as a tool to teach," he told me many years later. "I thought, 'This would be good for our game.' And so we used to sneak it out of school at night and I'd get a couple of kids to run the equipment."

Mike Kasmetis was a goaltender for Neilson in Peterborough. He also toils at Roger's summer hockey camps as part of the medical staff. "He got a one-inch videotape machine from the CHEX-TV station," says Kasmetis. "You couldn't even tell the teams apart. There was no fast forward, or rewind, but he'd tell us to watch for the play coming up and we were mesmerized by it."

One of Neilson's other innovations was to add dry-land training to hockey. Into the 1970s, players were expected just to show up at camp and play themselves into condition. Neilson, a physical education teacher by profession, loved nothing better than to apply his school-board-issue whistle and a stopwatch to put his Petes through their paces. The traditional Neilson run was along the concession roads in Otonabee–South Monaghan Township, southeast of Peterborough. According to Kasmetis, who was with the Petes from 1972 to 1976, Roger would have his players running ten miles a day in training camp – five in the morning and five in the evening.

The Neilson Five-Miler had legs, it turns out. The tradition was picked up by long-time Petes coach Dick Todd in the 1980s, and in the spring of 2004, after the Petes missed the playoffs, the team took the unusual step of holding a two-week mini-camp to kick-start the next season. And the old Neilson route was used for daily runs by players, while a couple of Neilson's guys, GM Jeff Twohey and assistant coach and GM Darren Keily, supervised.

According to Petes lore, Dallas Eakins holds the record for the fastest time, completing the five-mile route in about twenty-seven minutes.

Once he got his kids back in the arenas, Roger was up to his old tricks. Like the time he took the 1972 Petes to the Memorial Cup tournament. In the semifinal against the Edmonton Oil Kings, Neilson twice asked for third-period stick-blade measurements on Oil Kings players. The game was tied 4-4 at the time. Both sticks were found to be illegal, the Petes scored on one of the ensuing power plays, and won the game 6-4.

Edmonton was livid about Neilson's tactics. "They're sick," said Oil Kings general manager Bill Hunter. "It's the cheapest way I know to win a hockey game."

"I know it's a cheap penalty for the Memorial Cup," said Neilson. "I didn't call it."

With his own team, Neilson had more gimmicks than a carny. He'd hold competitions at practice. The winner would get a chocolate bar the coach placed on the boards. Mike Kasmetis says the players would "kill ourselves for a ten-cent chocolate bar."

Dick Todd recalls how the twenty-five-cent bribe to see who could lay down ten straight practice bunts became fifty cents per hit in junior hockey. "If you hit Denis Potvin seven times, it was worth $3.50," says Todd. "Roger would subtract from a player's fine totals. He started fining players a dollar if they were on the ice for a power play goal against. It got up to seven dollars for one player. I remember in one game, he'd already been on the ice for a goal when the guy skated over to the bench on a power play situation and said to Rog, 'If you don't mind, I think I'll pass on this one. I can't afford it.'" Players only earned $10.99 per week at the time, according to Kasmetis.

Long before he reached the NHL, Roger could upstage a referee. Former Petes goaltender Greg Millen recalls a night in Oshawa in the mid-1970s when team captain Doug Jarvis was penalized for

swearing at or near an official. Now, Jarvis might have been the one player on Roger's roster incapable of uttering profanity, so Neilson went ballistic. He sent his players, one by one, over to the penalty box until it was overflowing with Petes. They looked like a 1950s frat house gang trying to cram into a phone booth.

"There!" said Roger to the referee as he yanked off his vest and waved it in the air. "You've got my team, do you want my vest, too?"

Rogers' friends and hockey fans usually can't tell a story about him without busting into a grin, but some of those Petes weren't laughing. Neilson was strict.

Most junior coaches in the 1960s, 1970s, and beyond thought that school and jobs were a distraction to their players. Neilson, the veteran teacher, not only insisted his players go to school, they had to show him their report cards and pay five-dollar fines if they were late for class. Multiple infractions often meant the swift end to a Petes career. In 1975, Roger had just three players who weren't students and they were asked to find steady work.

For *Weekend Magazine* in April of 1975, Chris Zelkovich wrote the quintessential story on Roger's junior hockey days, in which he outlined the discipline and structure Neilson instilled in the Petes organization, on ice and off. "There's no bumming in Peterborough," Neilson told Zelkovich. "We don't hire players to work in the arena or anything like that."

Curfews were enforced, and hockey was no excuse for being tardy or absent. "I'd like to go out after the game and have a couple of beers, but I have to be back home in an hour," winger Mark Perras said after a particular home game. "It bugs me. I'm nineteen and I should be able to run my own life. But I guess when you think about it, it really does make sense."

Rick MacLeish, a Lindsay boy who went on to a fine NHL career, mostly with the Philadelphia Flyers, told Zelkovich that

Neilson had a way of being firm without sounding authoritarian. "When I was there, we'd get in from Montreal at 5:00 a.m. and still have to be in school that day. It sounds tough, but nobody really minded."

Jarvis played four years under Neilson and they remained friends for life. As a junior, Jarvis said that teenagers relished strong guidelines, even if they grumbled about them. "When someone's checking up on you, you know someone cares – and to guys away from home, that means a lot."

It meant a lot to the folks back home as well.

"No parent was worried about sending his kid to the Petes, knowing what Roger stood for, his integrity, the values he had, and then his hockey expertise on top of that," said Jarvis. "I always felt Peterborough was one of the best places to go.

"You knew what the expectations were with Roger. He had a tutor for us if we needed help in school. He kept on top of our marks all the time. You were held accountable, whether you were in school or had a job."

In 2003, Jarvis was named head coach of the AHL Hamilton Bulldogs, the top farm team of the Montreal Canadiens. As a working professional coach, Jarvis can't help but think about the most influential hockey instructor he knew. "I appreciated his coaching, but also what he stood for as a person," he says. "I learned a lot from him. You were fortunate as a young person to have him as a coach with the program he ran. When I think of how I miss him, it's his friendship I miss most of all."

Considering Neilson used to use old Russian hockey-training manuals with his young charges and always kept an open mind about global hockey, it was a thrill for him to take his Peterborough Petes to Russia to compete in the 1974 world junior championships. These were the days of innocence in world junior play, before it became a multi-million-dollar business deal, before it was even an official tournament. It was the first unofficial world junior tourney,

at Leningrad, just two years after the famed Canada–Russia Summit Series of 1972.

The Russians were loaded – seven players on the team would go on to win Olympic or world-championship gold medals. And here was "Canada," represented by a club team. Peterborough wasn't even the best junior team in the province of Ontario. So for Neilson's club to return with a bronze medal was further evidence of Roger's defensive systems at work.

"Russia was a great adventure," says Todd, Neilson's trainer at the time. "Roger was always watching the Russians practise. He was building up his base of knowledge, always trying to learn. That was my first year with the Petes. The year before, Roger had a great team, but he'd lost most of them, and this was a pretty young group. To make things worse, most of the team came down with giardia and it was lucky that one of the dads was a doctor."

Roger returned to Canada and the OHA, but his junior days were numbered. Having been to a Memorial Cup and, later, having faced the mighty Russian teams, Roger was ready to turn professional.

CHAPTER 3

Off to the Pros

Roger Neilson always said he didn't aspire to holding the keys to an NHL office.

He was just as happy coaching the juvenile Keene Expos, the peewee Bick's Pickles, or the Peterborough Petes. When he got fired from his seventh NHL head coaching gig, for the crime of contracting cancer, Neilson said he could easily go to coach the Lindsay Muskies provincial Junior A team. He owned the club, after all, so he could certainly get an interview. He might have found, finally, a bit of job security, unless he felt obliged to fire himself.

All of this modest ambition (coaching is coaching, he said) didn't take the shine off his first days in the only hockey arena that truly mattered to a young Toronto boy. Before he coached his first game at Maple Leaf Gardens in 1977, Neilson sat in the stands all by himself in the palace built miraculously by Conn

Smythe during the Great Depression, and drank it in till he got drunk from the feeling.

"It never really hit me until one day around the end of training camp I was walking through the end reds behind the net and I stopped and said to myself, 'Hey! I'm the coach of the Maple Leafs,'" Neilson told the *Globe and Mail*.

"I remember in grade 3 we used to get conduct reports every week to take home to our parents. They gave us a 'yes' or a 'no' on whether you'd been a good boy. If I had a 'no,' my punishment was that I couldn't listen to the Leafs game [broadcast by Foster Hewitt] on the radio. It was the worst thing that could happen.

"When I was in grade 5 or 6, we used to come to the junior doubleheaders on Saturday afternoon. First the Marlies would play, then St. Michael's. Then, we'd hide in the washrooms, five or six of us. The guards would come around to check but we would stand on the toilet seats so when they looked under the door they couldn't see us, and that got us in for the Leafs game, too."

But the Gardens would not be Roger's first home as a pro coach.

In 1976, Neilson left the Petes – not exactly kicking and screaming, but mildly intrigued at the possibility of making an entry into professional hockey, one that would mean a decent raise from his $30,000 salary. His first assignment, which, given the overall record, turned out to be like pulling into the pits to change tires, was in Dallas, Texas. Word of Neilson's remarkable record in the amateur ranks, twenty-five years of coaching winning baseball and hockey teams, had a wider circulation than Roger's old paper route. In a decision approved by the Chicago Blackhawks and Toronto Maple Leafs, Neilson was hired to run the Dallas Blackhawks, a Central Hockey League affiliate shared by the two NHL teams.

A young woman named Nancy Nichols was working in the Dallas offices when Roger, the new coach and GM, entered, leaving a lasting impression somewhere between shock and awe. "Roger

walked into the office, and the first thing he said was, 'Where do you have to go to get a decent bowl of soup around here?' " says Nichols. "My first job with Roger was finding him soup.

"Then he said he wanted a videotape machine. It was going to cost $1,800. I was making $400 a month at the time, and Roger was earning less than $40,000."

Neilson grumbled to the Dallas office staff about having to give up his paper route to go down there.

"We all looked at each other, like, o-kaaaaaay," says Nichols. "Roger had just turned forty-two, he had these big muttonchops and the big Afro, and he's talking about paper routes and hockey bingo. It was like Bill Veeck walked into the room."

Veeck, the late owner of the Chicago White Sox, was renowned for his marketing stunts.

"Roger had all these ideas, on and off the ice. He knew he had to sell hockey."

Considering bingo was illegal in Texas, they all wondered how Neilson didn't get arrested. "We were doing ten-cent beer night and bingo," says Nichols. "We had a bunch of drunken people playing bingo. It was perfect."

By now you know the Neilson modus operandi, so you won't be surprised to hear that Neilson, his staff, and friends would play ball hockey or shinny in the wee hours after the crowd thinned out. The arena, a livestock coliseum, was a hellhole, and that's putting it kindly. Roger tried to pull his skate on one morning, but couldn't until the rat occupying it had scurried away.

Though he was there for only a year, Neilson made connections in Dallas that would last a lifetime. Mike Pelyk, in the twilight of his playing career, was with the CHL Hawks that year. So were John Anderson and Randy Carlyle, on their way up, and a young defenceman named Mike O'Connell, now GM of the Boston Bruins.

Leafs GM Jim Gregory was impressed with Neilson's work with his prospects in Dallas, so when owner Harold Ballard fired

Red Kelly as head coach in Toronto, Roger was the logical replacement. Neilson's first NHL contract consisted of a note handwritten by Gregory. There was no negotiation. Ballard paid him $40,000 a season on a two-year deal. Neilson was so happy to get the opportunity he would have worked for nothing.

It didn't take Roger long to make significant changes to the Leafs. He was quickly poring over video evidence of Kelly's Leafs, looking for fatal flaws, and he didn't have to look very hard.

Neilson saw a Toronto team that was out of position and out of condition. Weeks before training camp, he was in touch with his players, outlining a physical training regimen they were to undertake prior to camp. That's standard procedure today. Then, it was revolutionary. By the time they arrived at camp, Neilson's players were running five miles in under thirty-five minutes and beginning to wonder if they were preparing for the Toronto Marathon. Everything about the Leafs was new and different with Roger as coach. NHL teams of the day spent endless hours engaging in scrimmages. Neilson cut them back and inserted competitive drills in their place. "Scrimmages," he said, "can become a breeding ground for bad habits." He invented showdown competitions and kept track of the results. Players checked them and started to worry if they were trailing on the list.

The *Toronto Star* described Neilson as having "ideas and approaches far removed from the dull, old notions of the majority of coaches whose only preparation for a complex job was to play for coaches with the same dull, old notions."

Neilson demanded defensive responsibility from his forwards and defence and monitored the Leafs' individual and team play in ways the players hadn't experienced before. The coach kept track of faceoffs won and lost, giveaways, scoring chances for and against, bodychecks given and missed. All of these are accepted tools of analysis in modern hockey; for NHL players in 1977, they were eye-opening developments. Some players grumbled at the sudden

accountability demanded by Neilson, others loved the feedback, a few were in shock.

With laborious, painstaking effort, Neilson broke down hours of game video on a primitive reel-to-reel system and showed the players their highlights and lowlights. "He had to be a contortionist sometimes to edit tape, one hand doing one thing and the other something else," says Neilson's assistant coach Ron Smith. "I don't know how he did it, and he was probably the only one who could do it."

Assistant coach. That was another bold Neilson stroke, hiring an assistant. No such animal existed in the NHL of the 1970s. Ballard thought it was folly and refused to acknowledge Smith's existence. Gregory relented because Neilson kept pushing to have a helping hand, and mind.

Neilson knew Smith from the Ontario Hockey Association. He had been the OHA's first technical director and often brought in Neilson to instruct at coaching clinics. "When Roger got the job in Toronto, he said he wanted to have me as an assistant," says Smith, who now coaches the Lowell Lock Monsters of the American Hockey League. "I said, 'Well I have an office on Jarvis, about two blocks from the Gardens, so I'll help out when I can.' I was also coaching Guelph of the OHA at the time."

For two seasons, Smith attended all the Leafs practices and most of their games. He was paid the grand sum of $5,000 per year, plus a pair of tickets to every Leafs home game.

"There were probably a million people in Canada who would've traded places with me and would today," says Smith. "It was a tremendous experience."

Smith marvelled at Neilson's work behind the game bench, including his unusual fascination with line combinations and the groundbreaking analysis that followed. "It was like a marriage of science and the arts," he says.

Roger videotaped every Leaf game. He studied the tapes, boiled them down to a version for player viewing, and used what he saw

as the basis for a handwritten report he would post in the dressing room the next morning. It didn't matter if Neilson had to stay up half the night to write it. Of particular concern to the coach were giveaways and missed assignments.

"I don't think Ian Turnbull liked those reports too much," says Smith of the Leafs' offensive-minded defenceman. But Ron Ellis, the team's responsible two-way winger, loved the feedback. "He would give positive reinforcement when you did something well and was balanced when you blew it and let your man score," says Ellis, now director of public affairs for the Hockey Hall of Fame. "There was constructive criticism, but it was also positive."

At times, Neilson asked his players to be students. Goaltenders Mike Palmateer and Gord McRae had to submit written reports after games detailing how goals were scored against them and what they might do to stop them in the future. The process was designed to keep his 'keepers on their toes while building up a book on enemy shooters, as a pitcher would in baseball.

Because Neilson personally scouted his opponents whenever possible, he knew as much about his rivals as any NHL coach, and he shared those insights with his players.

"We'd have meetings before a big game and he'd make it very clear what our roles were," says Ellis. "I liked that. On a particular night, he might say to the Darryl Sittler line, 'We're going to go power against power.' So he might say to my line, with Walt McKechnie and Dan Maloney, 'We're going to need a goal or two,' or, 'All I want from you is to shut down this line.' You went into the game prepared, and I really liked that sort of coaching technique."

Neilson quickly established a reputation for being a player's coach. He created a committee on the Leafs, comprising Sittler, Ellis, Turnbull, Lanny McDonald, and Borje Salming. They would meet with Neilson and make suggestions on travel itinerary and practice schedules. They might express a player concern, and act as a liaison between the room and the coach's office. While

Neilson had the final say, the players appreciated having a voice.

Later, however temporarily, that committee would help save Neilson's job.

Neilson threw himself into his first NHL job like a junkie into a fresh supply. He was relentless. All the extracurricular hours and activities he'd created and manufactured were saved up like pennies and poured into the Leaf cause.

Canadian magazine profiled Roger with a look at a typically insane week in his life.

It's 12:40 a.m. and, in a hotel room high above Montreal, Roger Neilson is looking rotten. Wearing only a pair of slacks, he's sprawled in a chair in front of the TV set, a soggy Kleenex in one hand. The picture is on, but the sound is turned down. Roger Neilson squints at the picture through eyes that are red and sore. His nose is red, too. And dripping. He dabs at his nose with the Kleenex. When he isn't sniffing pitifully, he's yawning noisily. His breathing is heavy and congested, like that of a broken-nosed prizefighter.

It's now Friday and Roger Neilson hasn't slept since Tuesday night. But he doesn't complain. He doesn't care. It's how he wants it. Roger Neilson is a man possessed. He hasn't stopped running since June of last year when he was named coach of the Toronto Maple Leafs, succeeding the sincere but aloof Red Kelly, who was fired.

Day and night, Roger Neilson runs. He seldom eats, sleeps, or socializes. He's consumed by a burning passion, to accomplish this year what no Maple Leaf coach has been able to do in the past 10: return the Stanley Cup to Toronto.

It's an arduous and taxing mission. Wednesday night, he was in St. Louis where the Leafs beat the Blues 4-3. Thursday morning at 4 o'clock, the Leafs arrived back in Toronto. The players went home to bed. Roger Neilson went to his office.

There, he pored over his game notes, analyzing areas of strength and weakness, devising strategy for future encounters.

At 8 a.m., Roger Neilson went back to his hotel apartment near Maple Leaf Gardens. He shaved, showered, changed clothes, had a bite to eat – and returned to his office. He ran a videotape of the St. Louis game, dissecting carefully, making notes. He did this for three hours. At noon, Roger Neilson went back to his apartment. He packed a small leather overnight bag with his shaving kit and an alarm clock. He then got in his car and drove to a suburban arena where he led the Leafs in practice. After the practice, he gave the players an hour of classroom instruction.

Shortly before 5 p.m., Roger Neilson left the arena, got in his car, and drove to the airport. He caught a 6 p.m. plane to Montreal. During the flight, he made notes on the practice. In Montreal, he took a taxi to the Forum where he scouted the 8 o'clock game between the Canadiens and the Buffalo Sabres. He made notes.

At 11 p.m., Roger Neilson took a taxi to the Sheraton Mount Royal Hotel, checked in and went to his room. He put the shaving kit in the bathroom and the alarm clock on the bedside table. He set the alarm for 5 a.m. He turned on the TV set and collapsed in a chair, fighting a cold and exhaustion.

At 5 a.m., Roger Neilson will get up, shave, shower, and take a taxi to the airport. At 7 a.m., he will get on a plane and fly to Philadelphia. At 1 p.m., he will scout the holiday game between the Philadelphia Flyers and the Cleveland Barons. He will make notes.

At 5 p.m., he will get on a plane for Toronto. He will go over his notes. At 6 p.m., he will land, get in his car and drive to his office. There, he will arrange his notes, charts and deep into the night, work on his master plan to make the Toronto Maple Leafs the best hockey team in the world.

How long can Roger Neilson go on this way before he drops? In a wasted voice, he says: "I promised myself that I would give it every ounce of strength this season and see what happens. That's what I'm doing and so far, so good."

The legendary yarn of Roger's Toronto bachelor days centred around a book that was found, standing upright, on one of his refrigerator shelves. It was a lonely book, accompanied only by a bottle of orange juice. An apocryphal story has Al Dunford, one of Neilson's former Peterborough rats who became Roger's travel secretary and statistician with the Leafs, placing the book in the fridge to see how long it would be before Neilson noticed it. Allegedly, the book was cold type for five months.

Dunford denies placing the book there, but does remember seeing it. He figures the man himself put it there. "Like all intense, thinking people, Roger could be so obsessed with the job at hand, he could be absent-minded," says Dunford. "He might forget where he parked his car. I think [former New York Islanders coach] Al Arbour was a bit like that."

Nancy Nichols confirms the Neilson lifestyle as described by *Canadian* magazine. Nichols and Neilson "fell in like," she says, during their time together in Dallas. At some point during his first season as Leafs coach, Roger invited Nancy up to Toronto to visit him, an invitation that evidently slipped his mind, or at least got lost in the maelstrom of Roger's life.

"The first time I came to Toronto, I was a nervous wreck," says Nichols. "I'd never been out of the States. Roger and I hadn't seen each other all that much, so it was a big commitment to go up there, and I was all excited. He was coaching the Leafs, and I was a big Leafs fan before that because of their Dallas connection.

"I got off the plane at the airport and a kid was waiting for me. A rat. It was Al Dunford. He took me to this high-rise apartment downtown. Roger had this bachelor pad with three

bedrooms in it, and the only thing inside it was orange juice. That was basically all he had wherever he lived. The places were all furnished and he just threw stuff in the medicine cabinet.

"So, I get to his place and Al says, 'Rog had to go to Boston to scout a game.'

"Now this is a head coach. But he had to go scout a game. Al was real nervous and he said, 'I think he'll be back tonight.'

"So, I waited. He didn't come back that night. Ron Smith, his assistant, was living there, too. He asks me what I'm doing here. I said we had this planned for a long time, I was coming up to see Roger. And Ron says, 'Well, he's gone to New England for four days. . . .' What?

"So I was there for four days before he showed up. It was cold. I think he might have been snowed in in Boston. And I was miserable."

Roger's impact on the Maple Leafs was profound. Inheriting a team that was one win above .500 in 1976-77, he directed the Leafs to their first forty-win season in twenty-seven years. They finished 41-29-10 and reduced their goals-against mark to 237 from 285.

In the playoffs, Toronto fans got their first taste of a third-round series after the Leafs breezed past the Los Angeles Kings and outlasted the rising New York Islanders, taking game seven on an overtime goal by Lanny McDonald in Long Island. Though the dynastic Montreal Canadiens swept the Leafs in the 1978 Stanley Cup semifinals, Neilson's Leafs made a spectacular splash. McDonald's overtime goal sent a buzz through Leaf Nation that would last through the spring. And the rookie coach had captured a second-round playoff series for the first time since the Leafs' Stanley Cup season of 1967.

Ellis was on that team; he had come out of retirement in 1977-78 only because he had heard Neilson was arriving as the new coach. Doug Jarvis and others had spread the word of Neilson's coaching abilities, innovative ideas, and human qualities.

"I was fortunate enough to play on a great team in 1967," says Ellis. "That was my third year in the league, and I was never able to match that feeling of being a part of something special until the year with Roger. There were a lot of frustrating years there for me. Sometimes it's hard to motivate yourself when you already know in training camp that you're not going to be competitive. But in '78, we knew we were close."

Unfortunately for Ellis and the rest of the Leafs, Harold Ballard didn't share that prescient view. Late in Neilson's second season with the Leafs, Ballard's buffoonery scaled new heights in an episode that would go down as one of the most bizarre in the rich history of the franchise. The paper-bag story has been told a thousand times in a thousand ways, but this is Neilson's detailed version of events, as told to Dick Irvin for his book on NHL coaches, *Behind the Bench*.

"We lost in Montreal on a Thursday night," Neilson told Irvin. "After the game, Harold Ballard told the TV announcers that he was going to fire me. I asked our GM Jim Gregory and he said, 'Yeah. You're done.'

"The next morning in Toronto I went down to the Gardens to clear out my stuff and all the players were there plus about a million reporters. But not one person from the Leafs management was there. Not one. I told the reporters we'd have a press conference at noon. I assumed somebody would be there by that time. Some of the players went out for a skate and the ones who were interviewed said the usual things they say when a coach is fired. By noon there still wasn't anybody there from the front office. So I had to announce my own firing. It was a bizarre situation."

Eddie Johnston was rumoured to be coming in from the Leafs farm team in Moncton. Neilson was contemplating a spur-of-the-moment offer from local radio station CKFH to do some colour analysis on their upcoming Leaf broadcasts. Behind the scenes, two

potential coaching candidates, Leafs scout and future GM Gerry McNamara and former coach John McLellan, had declined offers to take over the club.

Some of Neilson's players, including Sittler, McDonald, and Tiger Williams, had gone to Ballard and asked him to reinstate Roger, especially as the owner didn't have a ready replacement.

"That night I was still hanging around the dressing room and Ballard came in," said Neilson. "He always went there Friday evenings to have his toenails cut by the trainer. He said to me, in his usual gruff way, 'What are you doing this weekend?' I told him I didn't have any plans and he said, 'Don't go away. We may need you here.' That was his way of saying I was back in."

Dunford was disbelieving. "As Roger's friend, I felt it was my job to help him with his denial. I said, 'Give up the thought of coaching. It just doesn't happen in pro sport.' When was the last time a guy was fired on Thursday and rehired on Saturday?"

About a quarter-century ago, now. At Make Believe Gardens.

Though it didn't happen as simply as that. Ballard was lapping up the sudden rush of publicity the way he lapped up scoops of ice cream. While Neilson was feeling confident he'd retained his job, in the hours leading up to the Saturday *Hockey Night in Canada* broadcast of the Leafs game against the visiting Philadelphia Flyers the Leafs hadn't announced anything. Speculation was building that Roger might return to the bench, but Neilson himself was ducking the media.

"There's a million places you can hide in the Gardens."

A Jacuzzi being one of them.

The *Globe and Mail*'s William Houston, author of a biography on Ballard and *Inside Maple Leaf Gardens: The rise and fall of the Toronto Maple Leafs,* recently wrote this item involving Ralph Mellanby, then head of *Hockey Night*, and the night in question. A few hours before game time, Mellanby walked by the Leafs dressing room and saw Neilson in the Jacuzzi.

"What are you doing here?" Mellanby asked.

"I'm coaching the team tonight," said Neilson.

Mellanby said he relayed the news to *Hockey Night* producer Bob Gordon and host Dave Hodge but was met with disbelief.

Mellanby told them, "Roger Neilson never lies to anybody."

Jim Gregory, meanwhile, had been in touch with Neilson, telling him that Ballard was keen on milking the publicity surrounding the mysterious firing. Roger said that he didn't care, so long as he got his team back.

But then Gregory was on the phone to Neilson again. "What Harold wants to do is have you go out behind the bench during the national anthem and have a paper bag over your head."

The Unknown Coach gag.

Roger was taken aback by the suggestion.

"Well, he is giving you your job back," said Gregory. "Why don't you just do it for the reporters and then, when you get to the bench, take it off."

Neilson said he would.

And he might have, except that he bounced the idea off some of his friends and one of his key staffers, Al Dunford. Leave it to Roger to run with the advice of a twenty-four-year-old. Sage advice, as it turned out.

"You're coming out of this looking pretty good," Dunford told Neilson. "You can't join the circus."

Dunford remembers telling Neilson that he was "in the driver's seat," because Ballard had no options at this point.

"Al never liked Harold," Neilson told Irvin. "Harold had fired him three times, mainly because he wouldn't wear a tie. Anyway, I realized he was right and now it's getting on past 7:00 and the game starts at 8:00."

Neilson went to Gregory's office to tell him the bag caper was off. Just then, Ballard walked in and Neilson informed Harold himself.

"He didn't seem to mind too much," said Neilson. "He was just happy there had been all the speculation and publicity."

Happy to have had a diversion as well. Dunford believes Ballard was embarrassed at how the firing had been botched. The boss had assumed a loyal work hand like McLellan would jump at the job if asked, and the mystery surrounding Neilson's status was a welcome smokescreen to what Dunford calls "a comedy of poor management."

As game time approached, Roger, with McNamara, took the back route toward the Leaf players' bench. Though he resisted Harold's circus act, Neilson was nevertheless at the centre of a high drama on national television. During the national anthem, the camera panned to the coachless bench. Neilson walked along the corridor behind McNamara, and at the last second McNamara turned away and Neilson continued out to the back of the Leafs bench. The Gardens, and living rooms across the nation, erupted in applause. Flyers centre Bobby Clarke backed away from the faceoff circle to let the ovation live a little longer. It lasted nearly two minutes.

"All the people who wanted me fired two days before were now all solidly in my corner," said Neilson.

Not that they could save him at year's end. After a second-round sweep by the Canadiens – despite the fact that Montreal was on its way to another Cup and the Leafs pushed them to two overtime games – the Neilson era was over in Toronto. The Leafs had dipped eleven points in the standings from the ninety-two-point effort in Roger's debut season, and Ballard saw an excuse to dump the popular coach.

In retrospect, it was just one in a long line of ill-advised moves by Ballard. The 1980s were a disaster for Toronto. Punch Imlach returned from the old school as coach and declared war against the players who were close to Neilson. Ballard and Imlach traded McDonald to punish Sittler. It would be seven years after Roger left

before the Leafs would again reach the second round of the playoffs.

The face of Ron Ellis grows sad just thinking about the paper-bag night and the long years that followed. "I'm a Leaf through and through," says Ellis. "It's the only team I played for. I was with the Toronto Marlies. My father was a Marlie. There's a real connection. And I must admit that at the time [of the paper-bag caper] I was embarrassed being a member of the Toronto Maple Leafs. I could not believe that this organization I would die for was going through this scenario. It was a difficult time to say the least. For all of us.

"The tradition was damaged, stained, tainted. It took a whole new regime to come in and re-establish some of that tradition. You have to give some credit to Cliff Fletcher [president and GM from 1991 to 1997]. He came and made the organization respectable. There's no excuse for the Toronto Maple Leafs to not be competitive."

Media in Toronto loved Neilson and his Captain Video image. He was good copy. His players loved him. He treated them with respect. And all of this goodwill probably conspired against him.

"I wonder if Roger's demise in Toronto wasn't because he was getting more press than Harold," says Ellis. "Harold didn't like that. This was Harold's town. He didn't want the coach getting it.

"Maybe we were part of it, because all of us were speaking so highly of Roger. We were giving him the credit. Maybe Harold was upset with that. I really don't know. But every time a player was interviewed he would mention Roger."

Dunford was right. Neilson did come out of the Ballard big top looking good. He kept his dignity, if not his job. After the season, Ballard fired the bunch: Gregory, Neilson, Ron Smith, and the travel secretary Dunford, whom Ballard referred to as the "f—ing cruise director." All four learned of their fate through the media.

Roger had to drive up to Ballard's place at Thunder Beach, north of Toronto on Georgian Bay, to find out if it was true.

In his Christian manner, Neilson refused to speak ill of anyone, using humour to deflect the meanness of others. Harry Neale called it "Roger's gift." Surely Ballard was the acid test for the man's tolerance.

"He wasn't that bad, you know," Roger would say of his old boss.

Still, Roger got the last laugh when he was inducted into the Hockey Hall of Fame in 2002. From the dais, Neilson declared that there was one person who would have bet a million dollars against Roger reaching the Hall of Fame: "Harold Ballard. He'd be rolling over in his grave. Wherever you are Harold . . . up there, or maybe down there [he looked to the floor], I'm joining you, buddy. You and me together again, Harold." Neilson giggled, then he cocked his ear, pretending to listen to Ballard roaring at him from Hades.

"What's that?" said Neilson, returning to the mike to relay Hal's message.

"Harold said, down where he is, paper bags don't last very long."

BUFFALO SOLDIER

After his eventful two years in Toronto, Neilson wasn't out of a job for more than a day.

Roger and his agent, Rob Campbell, jumped in a car and motored to Buffalo for a meeting with Scotty Bowman, who had given Roger his first job in hockey. Bowman, then GM and head coach of the Sabres, wanted Roger to be his associate coach, but with a stipulation that he would become the head coach in year two.

Bowman suggested $50,000 as a fair salary.

"Okay, sounds good to me," blurted Roger.

Campbell quietly suggested to Roger that he go for a walk around the building while he negotiated a better deal. When Neilson heard he would be making nearly twice the initial offer, he

said to Campbell, "For crap's sake, that's pretty good. You probably want me to buy you dinner now."

Neilson walked into a solid situation in Buffalo. Or so it seemed. The expansion Sabres of 1970 had grown up, yet were still built around their first overall draft selection from their inaugural year, a slick centre from Victoriaville, Gilbert Perreault. In their tenth season, the Sabres were among the elite of the NHL. In 1979-80, with Scotty Bowman in his first season as GM and head coach and Neilson as his associate coach, the Sabres surged to a franchise-record 47 victories and 110 points, second in the league to the Philadelphia Flyers' 116.

Though the French Connection line of Perreault, Rick Martin, and René Robert was split up in October 1979 with Robert's trade to Colorado for John Van Boxmeer, there was plenty to get excited about in the city of chicken wings. Danny Gare emerged as a 52-goal scorer for the Sabres, Perreault enjoyed the second 100-point season of his career (106), and Martin was still a force. The trio combined for 141 goals and 274 points. In goal, Don Edwards and Bob Sauvé shared the Vezina Trophy in 1979-80, providing Bowman and Neilson with a reliable duo the coaches felt comfortable alternating.

One of the better public displays of the Sabres' offensive talent (only the Flyers and Montreal Canadiens scored more goals that season) took place on January 3, 1980, with Buffalo's 6-1 victory over the visiting Soviet Red Army at the Memorial Auditorium. Legendary Russian goaltender Vladislav Tretiak was in goal for the Red Army.

Expectations were that the Sabres would make their second visit to the Stanley Cup finals that season. Unfortunately, Bowman and Neilson ran headlong into the New York Islanders, the NHL dynasty that succeeded Montreal. After eliminating Vancouver and Chicago in eight games combined, Buffalo was rusty from a nine-day layoff and could do no better than stretch the Isles to a six-game semifinal.

The next season, as arranged, Neilson took over as head coach while Bowman concentrated on GM duties. It's difficult to imagine a better scenario than a strong team being run by two of the best minds in the game. Bowman, just forty-seven at the time, had coached the Canadiens to four straight Cups in the late 1970s and had learned the management side of the business from the master, Sam Pollock.

Bowman had hired Neilson, now forty-six, when he was coaching midget-level kids in Toronto, and had watched Roger develop into a bright tactician during a decade of coaching the Petes.

It should have been an ideal tandem. Harry Neale of *Hockey Night in Canada* says that if Neilson patterned his bench work after any coach, it was Bowman. Both were brilliant at matching lines and outmanoeuvring opposing coaches.

In reality, the ideal tandem was anything but. Bowman and Neilson were two strong-willed, stubborn hockey people, both of whom worked best when they had ultimate control. Bowman coached with what Al Dunford, who accompanied Neilson to Buffalo, described as a "flowing genius. It was in his head." Neilson recorded everything. Wrote copious notes, kept scrupulous stats. Broke down games and game videos.

Where they differed most was in their handling of people. Bowman was from the old school. He liked to keep his players guessing. He had an active doghouse and maintained an us-versus-them philosophy concerning a coach's relationship with his players. In comparison, Neilson ran a democracy. He felt that the coach and the players were all in it together, from the first-line star to the fourth-line plugger. In his continued admiration for two-way play, he came to appreciate the dogged talent of André Savard at least as much as the more stylish form of the original Sabre, Perreault.

Bowman felt that Neilson wasn't keeping him informed of developments with the team. "We don't have a normal coach-GM relationship," said Bowman to a reporter. "And we don't have the

same philosophy of coaching. I think players need a kick in the rear once in a while."

Beloved though he was, Neilson possessed an underrated ability to get under people's skin. He drove Bowman nuts. Neilson's agent, Campbell, claims Roger was "fired" three times by Scotty during the 1980-81 season, but the issue would always blow over.

Bowman's frustration with Neilson finally exploded in a Minneapolis hotel parking lot during the Sabres' ill-fated playoff series against the North Stars in the spring of 1981.

According to Neilson's version of events, at one point Scotty screamed at him, "You made André Savard our best player just to spite me. You're fired after this season, you're gone. I don't care if we win the Stanley Cup."

Bowman doesn't recall arguing over a particular player. And he insists he didn't want to lose Neilson at the end of the season, despite pressure from upper management to change the Sabres' style of play, make it more exciting.

Savard, who recorded 31 goals and 74 points that season, totals he wouldn't again approach in his career, says he looked out the window of his hotel room and saw Bowman and Neilson arguing.

"I was trying to sleep, and I opened up the curtain and saw them," says Savard, now assistant GM to one of Roger's Boys in Montreal, Bob Gainey.

"Roger told me later that I was a part of the conversation. It was funny, really."

Scotty wasn't laughing.

After the Sabres fell in five games to Minnesota, a distressing playoff loss considering the North Stars were twelve points below the Sabres in the regular-season standings, Bowman and Neilson parted ways.

Campbell was in Bowman's office to hear Scotty say he didn't fire Roger. When Campbell said that he *had* fired him, Bowman, according to Campbell, "lost it," he was so angry.

Neilson said later that the two had mutually agreed to part ways. And they remained good friends, once they stopped working together.

Curiously, just as the Leafs entered a dark period in the 1980s after Neilson left and Ballard and Punch Imlach demoralized and gutted the team, so, too, did the Sabres struggle after the two-year fling with excellence under Neilson. Between 1982 and 1992, Buffalo won one lonely playoff series, though it was memorable, a Bowman-coached special. The Sabres beat Bowman's old Canadiens team in a three-game sweep before losing a game-seven thriller, in double overtime, against Boston in the next round.

Thereafter, Buffalo looked to the late 1990s and a Czech goaltender named Dominik Hasek for the next bit of playoff glory.

As he arrived in Vancouver in 1981 to some left-coast thinking that suited his spirit, and weather that suited his bare feet, Neilson felt a little stung by his early experiences in the NHL coaching business. After ten relatively peaceful, secure seasons as a junior coach, he was like the kid who ran off to join the circus. First he gets fired by a foul-mouthed clown and then he's dismissed by the lion tamer, all in a four-year span.

In his brief NHL career, Neilson had already compiled a winning record and directed a handful of playoff-series victories, but he carried, and always would, a bit of that forever-young naïveté about him.

"Roger was an innocent in some ways," says Rob Campbell. "He felt that if you did your job and prepared as hard as you could, you would be successful. In the pro sports world, with its money and egos, that doesn't always work."

Summer was in full bloom when Roger arrived in Vancouver to breathe in the mountain air. The B.C. lifestyle could not have

been a better fit. He loved Vancouver. It was great for him, great for his dog, Mike. Neilson made his home in Deep Cove on the north shore, and he and Mike would frequently hike the Baden-Powell Trail. He could ride his bike to work.

Down at the office, a plan was in place. Jake Milford, the Vancouver Canucks GM, was close to retirement, and head coach Harry Neale was set to take his place in a year's time. Into this orchestrated scenario, Neilson arrived with the understanding he would work as a co-coach to Neale, his former Toronto playground pal, for the 1981-82 season, and become head coach the next season when Neale became GM.

As any armchair Canucks historian knows, that schedule was updated suddenly after a dramatic incident in Quebec City on March 20, 1982. The air in the quaint Colisée was always charged, but especially so when the Canucks pulled in, after a preceding date in Montreal against the Canadiens. Ragged Canucks winger Dave "Tiger" Williams, loved by his fans in Vancouver and Toronto and despised elsewhere, was well marked in Quebec for using the four-letter F-word to describe French Canadians.

So, when Williams started grappling with Nordiques legend Peter Stastny near the Vancouver bench, a notorious fan reached over the low glass along the boards of the Colisée to get at Williams. Neale, it turns out, knew of this particularly loud-mouthed fan from his World Hockey Association days and says he had often thought of walking up to the guy's seat and decking the SOB. So when the fan ran to the boards to reach Williams, the Canucks head coach reacted instantly. As described by Tony Gallagher and Mike Gasher in their book *Towels, Triumph & Tears: The Vancouver Canucks' Amazing Drive to the Stanley Cup Finals*, Neale switched from his more typical metaphysical defence of Williams to a physical defence. Neale, a former defenceman who played for the 1956 Toronto Marlboroughs, leaped into the crowd and threw a rather meaningful punch at the fan. The punch didn't land,

though, and Neale says he nearly put out his shoulder throwing it.

A wild scene ensued, with a few players, including Doug Halward and a future coach of the Canucks, Marc Crawford, following Neale into the stands. Neilson, meanwhile, ditched the headset he was wearing for communication with assistant coach Ron Smith upstairs and tried to bring order to what was taking on the look of a bar brawl.

Ultimately, while the Canucks would claim that *Le Cirque du Colisée* brought them together as a team, all it brought Harry Neale was a ten-game suspension from NHL president John Ziegler.

"I guess I should have hit a referee instead," cracked Neale, referring to the five-game suspension Philadelphia's Paul Holmgren received when he hit referee Andy van Hellemond.

As the Canucks' season continued on its fairy-tale ride, midnight pumpkin included, the Quebec City brawl came to be seen as the turning point for the team and became a bit of a sore point with Neale. As the club's head coach and future GM, Neale had every right to regain his team for round one of the playoffs against the Calgary Flames. The suspension applied to the regular season, not the post-season, but hockey people are among the most superstitious creatures on earth. They entertain painstaking rituals, from forgoing changes of underwear to dipping hockey sticks in the toilet bowl, in the hope of bringing luck. And they don't mess with what ain't broke, as Neilson himself would painfully learn a few years down the road in Philadelphia.

"It was a nothing move to not coach," says Neale today of his decision to stay away when the team was doing so well without him. Still, it bothered him, as it would any coach, to hand over his team on the eve of the playoffs. "It did," says Neale, "and I could have easily come back. But I thought, under the circumstances, why would I?"

Throughout the season, the gregarious Neale had been in the forefront, the gifted spokesman and leader, while Neilson quietly

performed the grunt work in the background, teaching and connecting with his players. Now, it was Neilson's show while Neale took an uncomfortable seat in the press box. Neilson did things his way, with a teacher's eye for classroom preparation. After the Canucks completed the regular season with four victories and a tie under their new head coach, Neilson handed each player a playoff folder, reminding him of certain tasks, a checklist of such Hockey 101 fundamentals as forechecking and breakouts. When he was coaching the Peterborough Petes, Neilson used to scribble out his list of "Ten Things You Don't Do When Leading a Game." From an earlier life as a baseball coach, Roger knew there was no substitute for preparation and repetition.

Neale was in awe of the lengths to which Neilson would go to keep his players enlightened.

"He would break down video after a game, which took six or seven hours with that early equipment," says Neale. "And he took great pride that when players came to the rink in the morning they had the up-to-date statistics on the video, because you didn't get the NHL stats like you get now. And that was on one of those big machines – you couldn't carry it on the road. Now, video is standard, and the video coach is as important as anybody else."

Just as extraordinary was Neilson's courageous approach to working with players. He brought to Vancouver the groundbreaking ideals of hockey democracy he'd fostered in Toronto and Buffalo. Punch Imlach didn't want to hear from a player unless he was spoken to, and even then it was fifty-fifty. Neilson inquired about players' families and personal well-being. He handed out questionnaires to his Canucks, seeking their preferences for practice times, game-day skates, game meals, and post-trip schedules. He asked the trainers for their input.

"Now he had to cut and send down players like we all did," says Neale. "And I know if I'd sent out a questionnaire like that when I was coach, a few of them would have said, 'This asshole

doesn't know what he's doing, or he's favouring people,' but with Roger there were no complaints other than a few guys saying there was too much video."

For the next little while, the video was more like a Hollywood movie called *Rocky*.

A sub-.500 team in the regular season, the Canucks were the gritty wonders of the world. They were on a roll that included a generous dose of the kind of good luck a playoff team needs. As usual in the early 1980s, the New York Islanders and Edmonton Oilers were the teams to beat. But in Vancouver's favour, the Los Angeles Kings delivered a massive first-round upset of Edmonton, and the Islanders wouldn't have to be dealt with until the final.

Getting there was made easier by the fact that the Canucks, a seventy-seven-point team in what was a relatively thin Campbell Conference that year, didn't face a playoff team that finished ahead of them in the standings. Not until the Islanders, anyway, and at the outset, who worried about such trivial stuff when the Canucks hadn't yet won a playoff series in the twelve-year history of the franchise?

The sweep of Calgary in the best-of-five opening round took care of that, an astonishing development considering the Canucks had lost captain and defenceman Kevin McCarthy to a broken ankle in a fluky accident at practice two days before the series opened.

"King Richard" Brodeur, who a decade earlier had led the Cornwall Royals to a Memorial Cup final victory over Neilson's Peterborough Petes, was truly regal against the Flames, and Neilson was just warming up with his bench work. Few coaches in the game (Bowman is one) cared as much about line matchups as Neilson. While he doubtless felt it helped his team to have the line he wanted against the enemy's top unit, line matching also kept the coach in the game. He loved baseball, remember, for the degree to which the coach is involved, having an impact on the outcome. Matching lines was Roger's game within the game, and few played it better.

In 2002, when Jacques Martin graciously stepped aside as head coach of the Ottawa Senators for the final two games of the season to allow Neilson to reach 1,000 games as a head coach, Roger's Peterborough pals rushed to congratulate him at the Corel Centre. Among the first things out of Roger's mouth: "I didn't miss a matchup all night."

A bit of perspective. This was a cameo appearance in a meaningless game by a coach about to be inducted into the Hall of Fame – and Neilson was focused on getting the line matchups he wanted. Perfect.

One of the advantages of coaching a team deep in muckers, like the 1982 Canucks, is that there was no shortage of checkers to sic on the scorers. Against the Flames, Neilson usually had Curt Fraser on Willi Plett, and Tiger Williams was all over his good friend and former Leafs teammate Lanny McDonald. When Williams delivered the overtime winner in game two, a backhander that beat Calgary goalie Pat Riggin, it ignited the Canucks and provided a rebirth to the veteran slugger after a difficult season.

Like so many others, Williams marvelled at Roger's hockey knowledge. "He tells us any time we have a better idea to come and tell him," said Williams. "But it's a hollow statement because he's heard any idea a hundred times before."

Neilson had home-ice advantage for the first three series, meaning he could make the last line change in the majority of games. With Brodeur playing the best hockey of his life and the Canucks checkers hounding the Flames, then the Kings, and finally, the Blackhawks, frustration set in on the opposition benches.

After taking down L.A. in five, the Canucks and Neilson made life miserable for Chicago head coach Bob Pulford and his star centre Denis Savard.

"He drove Pulford and Savard nuts," says Neale. "He had two checking lines and so he always had one to put out. Savard was

breaking his sticks coming off. And of course Pulford wanted to get away from it. It was masterful."

In game two of the series, it was the Canucks' frustration with an on-ice official that set up one of the most famous incidents of Neilson's life. While Toronto cherishes the faux Paper Bag Night, Vancouver will never forget Towel Power.

Neilson always insisted the moment happened spontaneously. His target was referee Bob Myers, who was monitoring a game so nasty – NHL supervisor of officials Frank Udvari would say later – that God couldn't have refereed to anyone's satisfaction.

The Canucks certainly weren't satisfied to be receiving what they believed was an unfair share of the penalties, combined with a Vancouver goal that was called back on a phantom offside. Blackhawks goaltender Murray Bannerman took a swipe at Curt Fraser, and when the dust settled after that mix-up, Vancouver was the only team penalized. Savard soon scored to make the score 4-1 Chicago, so Neilson decided the circumstances called for drastic action.

The game was lost – it wasn't as though a coach or any player could turn around a three-goal margin late in the third period – but there was time to stage a protest to score a psychological point before the next game. It started with a sit-down strike: Neilson told his players to stay on the bench and not report for duty at the faceoff circle.

Williams, an eight-year NHL veteran at that point, and familiar with Neilson's tactics, asked his coach what he was going to do. Neilson wasn't yet sure himself.

"We should throw all the sticks out on the ice," said Tiger.

"Nah, we did that before," said Neilson.

Ron Smith says he remembers he had been yelling "We surrender" to Myers during the game. Neilson might have heard him, subconsciously or not.

In any case, Neilson noticed towels hanging on the clothesline in the bench area of the ancient Chicago Stadium. He grabbed one off the line, put it on the butt end of Jim Nill's stick, and held it aloft over the boards. The white flag of surrender. Neilson held the towel like that until his shoulder ached, and still he couldn't get Myers's attention. Several other players followed suit, hoisting towels – Williams, Stan Smyl, Gerry Minor, and Lars Molin – but it wasn't until a couple of players skated over to tell the referee to take a look that he glanced over and ejected all the flag wavers.

"I had no idea what I was starting," said Neilson afterward, in something of an understatement.

After the journey home, the Canucks' United Airlines flight was pulling in to the gate at the Vancouver airport when an Air Canada 747 aircraft taxied past – and the pilot was waving a white towel in salute at the arriving Canucks. Here was a hint of what was to come: airport workers armed with towels, hundreds of fans waving towels, a Coliseum white with towels for game three.

And so Neilson contributed yet another innovation to the game of hockey. Towel waving. By now, every NHL team has had a towel night for fans. Some hand them out each spring for playoff series, with the team's logo, for the whiteout effect. The NHL Jets left Winnipeg in a white salute. And when Neilson himself coached his 1,000th NHL game, at the Corel Centre in Ottawa, the Senators handed out Roger Neilson towels to mark the occasion.

Given the short- and long-term impact of his white flag of defiance, neither Neilson nor the Canucks could begrudge the fines imposed by the league: $1,000 to the coach and $10,000 to the club.

As a certain credit-card ad might say: Towel Power – Priceless.

Years later, at their cottage properties in the Kawarthas, Pulford would share a laugh or two with Neilson over the

incident, but at the time Pulford accused the Canucks coach of committing a "completely classless" act.

Not surprisingly, the coach and his players kept a lower profile over the next few days, though Neilson couldn't entirely restrain his dry sense of humour. When he complained, mildly, about a tripping infraction in game three that went against Anders Eldebrink, Neilson muttered, "It was a funny call, but nothing to raise a towel about."

The rest of the series was relatively anticlimactic, with the Blackhawks dropping the final three games, two of them in Vancouver. So, too, was the Cup final a letdown, a cold coffee to the face after the great ride by Brodeur, Smyl, and associates. The Canucks pushed the Islanders to overtime in game one, blew a lead and lost by two goals in game two, and were out of gas by the time the series returned to Vancouver.

In the end, losing to the Islanders in the third year of their four-straight Cup run didn't diminish the magic of an unlikely twenty-two-game span that started with a brawl in the other end of the country. Until the trip to Long Island, Neilson's band of muckers, three games below .500 in the regular season, ran up a 15-2-1 mark over the final five games of the regular season and first three playoff rounds.

Despite the sudden end, the city of Vancouver was smitten with its team, rallying around the heroes during a grand public celebration involving more than a hundred thousand people – the kind of march other clubs experience only after they win a Stanley Cup.

"When the city said it wanted to have a parade, we all kind of looked at one another like, 'What for? We lost the damn thing,'" Brodeur told the Canadian Press.

Neale and Neilson had more than a few laughs about the bizarre and wonderful Vancouver spring of 1982. Roger used to tell Harry the team wouldn't have reached the final if Neale had gone back behind the bench. To which Neale would say, "I can't

argue that, Roger, but I can argue this. We would have fricken done something in the finals if I was coaching, instead of going out four straight."

In seriousness, Neale concedes the streak was brilliant. "Calgary was a great series, and we were luckier than they were, I guess. But Roger's coaching was a big reason we beat Chicago, especially, and L.A."

The secret to the Canucks' success that spring wasn't the towels waving overhead, but a group of twenty players playing over their heads. But there's a price to be paid when the players return to earth, the price of inflated expectations.

"It's tough when you're a Cinderella team," says Neale. "Look what's happened lately." Carolina, Minnesota, and Anaheim are among the upstart teams of the new millennium that surged to surprisingly strong playoffs, only to suffer a severe letdown the next season. All eyes will be on Calgary this season. "I remember Jake Milford telling us," says Neale, " 'Boys, don't judge your players on their playoff play. Many of them can't do it for eighty-two games.'

"Jake would say that players are like machines, and you're running the machine shop. You want to get them all going at the same clip, and out of the back door of the machine shop come victories. And if one or two or three of the machines get out of sync, you've got to repair them. Or some night, when it's dark, get them out the door and get a new machine.

"Roger was appalled by that analogy. He'd say, 'Machines? These are human beings.'

"Of course, it went against his feelings, but there was a degree of truth to it."

Neilson's Canucks went five games under .500 in his first full season as head coach and lost in the first playoff round to a Calgary team pleased to gain revenge. Past the halfway mark of the following season, with the Canucks nine games below .500, Neale, the GM, was growing weary of fending off the challenges

from owner Frank Griffiths. Griffiths wanted Roger's head, and he expected Neale to serve it up. Twice, Neale had talked Griffiths out of firing Neilson, but after a rout by St. Louis and a loss to the powerful Oilers, Neale returned to his room at Edmonton's Westin Hotel to see the message light flashing on his phone. It was Griffiths, calling from Hawaii. Neale phoned him back.

Griffiths knew the score and didn't much care to hear about the Canucks' valiant effort.

"Did you tell Roger it was over?" asked Griffiths.

"Well, Mr. Griffiths, we played really well . . ."

"Harry," said Griffiths, "there's no sense in two people losing their jobs over this one decision."

With that, Neale made the slow walk down the hallway to Roger's room. He'd fired coaches before, but not like this. Not a close friend like Roger.

"Are you sure?" said Neilson, after Neale broke it to him.

Neale assured him he was.

"Well," said Roger, "it's not like you're the only guy who's fired me."

As usual with Neilson, there was a funny escapade to lighten the crisis. J.P. McConnell, sports director at CKNW radio station in Vancouver, was a television reporter for CBC at the time. Coincidentally, a gang of football media and Canadian Football League coaches was also in Edmonton staying at the Westin for the annual CFL coaches' convention. At breakfast the next morning, Neilson ran into Jim Robson, the Canucks long-time play-by-play man. Over coffee, Robson said he'd heard that Neale had called a press conference for later that morning.

"Oh, Harry's probably going to fire the coach," Neilson said, so matter-of-factly that it sounded like some other coach was getting canned.

Robson was disbelieving, but hustled off to the press conference to hear Neale say Neilson was gone and that Neale would

coach for the balance of the season. He explained that this decision was sudden – Neale didn't even have his skates with him to use for the remaining practices on the road trip.

"The shock rattled through the team and also through the sizeable contingent of hungover media members who were in the Westin for the football function," remembers McConnell. "Reporters scrambled to catch some quotes from the fired coach, while I waited for a borrowed cameraman to arrive from the CBC Edmonton headquarters.

"Roger was his usual accommodating self, staying as long as everyone needed until every question had been answered. Then he excused himself to pack for the trip home – but I still had no cameraman.

"Finally the shooter arrives in the lobby just as Roger is checking out on his way to the airport, and to make sure he catches his plane he agrees to do the interview with us in the cab, on the move, going to the airport. We all pile in – lights, camera, action – and off we go on the twenty-five minute drive to the Edmonton International, filming along the way, and killing two birds with one stone.

"Then, with the interview done, Roger casually mentions that he has neither plane ticket nor credit card with him. So I gave him my credit card, he bought the ticket, and in return for that favour he took the filmed interview we had done with him to Vancouver, where Eric Dwyer was waiting to pick it up at the airport.

"And at the end of the day, I think the CBC ended up paying for Roger's plane ticket – it just didn't seem right to have him pay the bill."

Neilson's agent, Rob Campbell, had called Neale early that morning, wondering if it would help if Roger talked to Griffiths before the firing was announced to the media. Neale said, "No, you don't know what's been going on."

At the very least, Neale wanted to be able to assure Roger he'd get paid for the balance of his contract, which had a year and a

half to run. "If he doesn't take a job," said Griffiths, "you've got that promise."

Neale relayed that to Neilson, who seemed to understand. But once the hyperactive son of a doctor, always the hyperactive son of a doctor. Within two days, Neilson was in Los Angeles, breaking down videos for the Kings.

Griffiths stopped paying Neilson, Neilson's lawyers took Griffiths to court, and the coach won handily. The B.C. Supreme Court awarded Neilson $173,500 plus costs, which comprised $53,500 owing on the 1983-84 season and $120,000 for the next season. Griffiths's lawyers had argued in vain that Neilson's earnings with the Kings and then the Blackhawks, where he went on to work as an assistant coach, should offset any financial award to Neilson.

It would be five years before Neilson was handed a team of his own again. In Chicago, he worked alongside Bob Pulford and then served as a Blackhawks scout for a couple of seasons, expanding his base of hockey knowledge and learning of the off-season delights of Maui.

Quirks, Creations, Dogs, and Doglegs

The genius of Roger Neilson was born of a brain that rarely rested. Unfortunately, when his synapses did snooze, he was often behind the wheel of a car.

It helps explain why Roger always travelled with accomplices. On the freeway, especially, narcolepsy is best shared with friends, nervous friends, able to seize the wheel.

One doesn't paint a portrait of Roger with a simple palate of colours. The nuances require a full range of hues. The subject is comfortable in a full range of background settings. And he utterly refuses to be painted into a corner.

A lover of silly games, Roger himself could well be the source of a game called Paradox. These terms and more have been used to describe his unique condition:

Controlling/Creative
Annoying/Endearing
Conservative/Rebellious
Stubborn/Sympathetic
Demanding/Playful
Combative/Forgiving
Serious/Silly
Respectful/Barefoot
Brilliant/Naive
Detailed/Forgetful
Workaholic/Narcoleptic
Generous/Parsimonious
Principled/Devious
Rule maker/Rule breaker
Private/Public

He covered a lot of ground, did Roger Neilson, even when he was standing still.

Neilson has been rightly knighted as the technical wizard who invented video analysis in hockey; this same man once tried to change a TV channel with a calculator and identified a microwave in a store as a television. In his later years, Captain Video used to grumble, perhaps facetiously, that modern NHL video equipment was so complicated he couldn't use it any more and left it in younger hands. This from a man who imitated contortionists while painstakingly editing reel-to-reel film in the 1970s.

Long before it became standard practice, Neilson introduced physical training and game video to hockey players, striving to improve their output and quality of play. This same man loved to clog up the neutral zone and slow a game to a crawl in the name of a defensive, one-goal victory, a man who once said of his junior team, "Usually, the duller we get, the better we get."

He was a heavy contributor to the trapping, cautious style that is today's game. Perhaps not surprisingly, he could get a bit touchy about criticism of the neutral-zone trap. "The trap is the most misunderstood system in sports," he said. "It's just positional play where you try to stop the other team from getting over centre." At his coaching clinics, Neilson advised his fellow coaches not to draw attention to defensive hockey. And in one of his Hilroy notebooks used to outline the clinics' agenda was this message in Roger's handwriting, under the heading "Coaching Tips": "Don't push video publicly."

As a junior coach, Neilson used a dog on the ice to teach a forward to forecheck. Today, some of hockey's greatest minds believe the game in its defensive obsession has gone to the canines.

Neilson himself, in his final days, is said to have bolted up from a delirious sleep to declare, "What are we going to do about the game?"

Roger was pushing limits and turning rules on their head long before he arrived in the NHL to be christened Captain Video. He knew the good and bad of every rule. Sometimes, his mission was to exploit it for the benefit of his team. Sometimes, he would expose silly rules that he alone seemed to have taken the time to consider and to dismantle.

The hidden-apple trick from his sandlot baseball days wasn't so different from his decision in junior hockey to send extra players over the boards while killing off a penalty. Wouldn't precious seconds tick off, he figured, before he was called for too many men on the ice? And if his team was already two men short and playing with the minimum of three players, why not muck up the proceedings and eat up some more time? It's not as though officials could penalize him down to two players (instead, they later bolstered the rule by ordering a penalty shot for such violations).

Meanwhile, his team won that game, a playoff game, protecting a late lead with a little Roger rule play.

Similarly, where was it written that Neilson couldn't send out Petes defenceman Ron Stackhouse to defend against a penalty shot, rushing at the bewildered shooter and sweeping the puck away at the blueline? It wasn't written anywhere – that is, until Neilson's defiance sent the rule makers back to the drawing board to insert a stipulation that only goalies, not defencemen, may defend a penalty shot.

He once pulled his goaltender, but instructed him to casually leave his stick in the goal crease. The stick blocked a would-be goal. Hockey now has a rule against that, too.

Neilson had an encyclopedic knowledge of hockey's rule book, which was a good thing considering how many changes he effected in it. It was while in the OHL (then called the OHA) that Neilson developed many of the hockey innovations and rule twists that characterize his career. He used to study the little guide to kill time on those long junior bus rides. "I think every coach should read it every month or so," said Neilson. "It's embarrassing if something comes up [in a game] and you don't know about it."

Roger believed that "shots on goal," a standard statistic to measure a team's performance, was meaningless compared to what he called "chances to score." Furthermore, he could break down the scoring chances on his video analysis to show his players. Thus was born the hockey term "chances." Reporters curse Roger, gently of course, every time a losing coach claims his team "outchanced" the opposition. It came to be viewed as too convenient an excuse. Yeah, we lost, but we did outchance them.

Neilson more or less pioneered the entire statistical analysis of the game as it exists today. He was the first to monitor face-offs won and lost. He kept track of power play production and penalty-killing performance. He tracked hits and offered tiny cash rewards for delivering them. Way back in Peterborough, he had his

statistical tykes keeping track – manually – of the minutes played by each of his players. According to Al Dunford, one of Roger's first statisticians, he wanted to see each player's TOI (time on ice) after every period, know who's tired and who's not, so he could decide whether he was making the best use of his resources. Modern coaches, reporters, and fans monitor TOI as an indicator of which players are the most highly valued in a given game. Imagine one statistician doing that manually, for all five players on the ice.

It's all standard stuff in hockey. After a game, coaches, officials, reporters, and even players grab the summary that will have special team stats, shots, faceoffs, and minutes and shifts played. One could argue that the summary could come with a headline: Game Report Brought to You by Roger Neilson. Players and their agents cash in on these statistics, when they can, in salary negotiations.

Of course, the big daddy of all Neilson's innovations was the use of video as a tool to break games down and instruct players. In a one-sentence obituary, Neilson is, first and foremost, the video pioneer.

In Roger's second season with the Maple Leafs in 1978-79, the *Toronto Star* offered a Saturday feature on "Roger Video and His Magic Machines." This is how the newspaper described Neilson's video techniques:

Not so long ago the most sophisticated items in a hockey team's equipment bin were long johns and jockstraps. Nowadays, the modern NHL dressing room and environs may look like the control panel in *Star Wars*. Maple Leafs coach Roger Neilson, for instance, likes to be two and three deep in the electronic helpers he employs to keep a statistical diary of his team.

His equipment consists of three video cassette recorders, two Panasonic reel-to-reel recorders, two television sets, a big screen and a portable video tape recorder and camera. Neilson

says he once needed an entire reel of tape for a period of hockey but can now get an entire game on a cassette.

The equipment is set up in a small anteroom in the Gardens, across the corridor from the players' dressing room. Penalty killers, said Neilson, consult the tapes regularly, "but other players never go near it." The big screen is located in the gym where players do their stretching exercises. The video tape equipment is sometimes used here and also the players find it easier to do their exercises by watching a PT expert go through the routines on the screen.

Neilson will use the normal TV feed of a game but usually prefers to have someone shoot a game for him to get the enlarged coverage he prefers. TV rarely shows the entire ice surface. Also, in some situations, he likes to isolate on a certain player. John McGillivray of CKFH does much of the camera work for Neilson, but for some games students are hired.

Neilson explained that video was essential to explain the strengths of an opponent, for example, the techniques and tendencies of a particular penalty-killing duo. Quite simply, he also needed a second look at a game he didn't always see that well the first time.

"You really don't see the complete game behind the bench," said Neilson. "Changing lines, especially if you're trying to match lines, is a full-time job. The other big parts of coaching to me are (b) strategy and (c) cheerleading. By cheerleading I mean telling a guy 'nice going' or giving him encouragement of some kind.

"Often you forget to tell a guy what a good play he made or you haven't the time. If he makes a mistake, though, you tell him and sometimes that's all the guys hear. If I didn't watch films I might miss a good play a guy made or vice versa."

Don Cherry, then coach of the Boston Bruins and now a broadcasting icon, scoffed at the use of video in the early years. "I see on the ice what Neilson sees on the video tape," said Cherry.

"I'm not knocking him. He came up a different way than I did. I came up like a blacksmith – from the bottom. I have a video tape machine at home and one in the office, but I look at them for enjoyment only, never when we lose. And I never look – for gawd sakes – to see where a guy is standing."

Not all of Neilson's video sessions involved hockey players in moments of greatness or great embarrassment. Occasionally, he used the tool as a means of inspiration. Eric Lindros recalled one memorable video session in Philadelphia.

"We were doing a video clip one day. We're playing the Leafs in the playoffs and we're going over where to shoot on Cujo [Curtis Joseph], how to break down their power play. All of a sudden he puts on the screen a flock of flying geese. His philosophy was, these geese can fly at 65 or 67 per cent less effort than it would take for them to fly alone."

Teamwork. Neilson was big on that, even if some people thought he was an odd bird.

Every genius has his foibles.

Einstein had bad-hair days. Van Gogh drank his paint and dropped an ear.

Roger was blessed with his own share of quirks. A comic could make a living out of spinning Roger anecdotes.

Most of the Roger stories stem from these general topics:
Driving and sleeping mishaps;
Golfing mishaps;
Boating mishaps;
Clothing issues;
Canine capers;
Absent-mindedness;
Parsimony.

CAUTION: SLEEPY DRIVER AHEAD

For a mentor who always had an ear for his players, Neilson frequently tuned out of conversations, never more famously than when Craig Ramsay, then a rookie with the Peterborough Petes, walked into Neilson's coach's office in 1967 to tell him he was homesick and quitting the team.

For days, the nervous sixteen-year-old Ramsay had been summoning the courage to tell Roger what was in his heart. He sat in the chair across from Neilson, started into his farewell speech and . . . *zzzzz* . . . Roger promptly dozed off.

"He sat there, with his back against the wall, sleeping," says Ramsay. "I didn't know what to do. I thought, 'I can't just leave.' Finally, he wakes up and says, 'Well, let's not do anything rash. Let's think about it a while.'

"He wanted me to stick with it, wanted some young players to build around."

Slightly perplexed, Ramsay left Neilson's office, stayed with the Petes, and went on to a long and successful hockey career as an NHL player and coach. Just another stroke of Neilson coaching genius?

Partly due to his long work days and early-morning habits, Roger was capable of falling asleep at any time.

When he was a teacher at Bayview Junior High, parents began to file in for teacher interviews. Sitting at his desk, ostensibly listening to an explanation of why Johnny doesn't always do his homework, Roger fell sound asleep in his chair. The astonished parents didn't know whether to wake him up or cover him up and leave the room. Moments later, he awoke and completed the discourse on Johnny.

Devin Smith, now of the NHLPA, who lived at Roger's house while attending Trent University in Peterborough, says it would take no end of coaxing to get Neilson to watch something on television

other than hockey. Finally, he might relent and agree to a movie.

Only one problem.

"The minute he sat down to watch it, he'd fall asleep," says Smith. "But he could watch hockey, including the late games, no problem."

In the mid-1990s, after being fired by the New York Rangers, Neilson toured New Zealand and Australia with Smith and Kent Pearce, sons of Neilson associates Ron Smith and Tom Pearce.

Nice idea, the tour, if only Roger would remember it's always safer when he's on the passenger side of the car. Maybe the location of the steering wheel threw him off?

"When we first got to Australia, we rented this old beat-up car, and remember, you're driving on the wrong side of the car and the wrong side of the road," says Pearce. "And it had a manual stick shift, on the steering column. So here's the three of us, not one of us knowing how to drive this thing. We got Rog in the seat and we took off out of the car-rental place, and he goes to make a left-hand turn, forgets he's on the wrong side of the road, misses a mailbox by inches. Now we're up on the sidewalk and people are scattering left and right. Roger stopped right on the sidewalk and got someone else to take over."

Roger loved Harvey's breakfast sandwiches, so much so that they affected his concentration. At a Harvey's drive-through in Ottawa, Neilson had *no* hands on the wheel while negotiating a sandwich and coffee. As if matters were not bad enough, he was exiting via a one-way entrance and slammed into a car driven by a startled and angry woman. Angry, that is, until she got out and recognized Roger.

Young friends Todd Ervin, Landry Smith, and his brother, Devin, were driving with Roger in Vancouver one time when he fell asleep

after stopping at a red light. The light turned green, and red again, before Roger woke up. Suddenly, he bolted awake and said, "What's wrong with this light that it's taking so long?"

The boys howled.

Many of his acolytes believe Roger would occasionally pretend to be dozing off on a trip so that a worried passenger would rush to take the wheel while the car was still moving. Broadcaster Greg Millen says Neilson crossed four lanes of the 401 near Toronto while dozing off. "I just yelled at him and wouldn't let him drive any more."

"I wouldn't let him drive," echoes Lynn Ervin, mother of Roger's dear friend Todd. "I'd been to visit him in Peterborough one time, and he was taking me to the airport in Toronto. I insisted on taking the wheel because I was afraid he'd fall asleep. I also remember driving through the streets of Toronto and people would recognize Roger and poke their head into the open window and say hi when the car was stopped at a light.

As if he didn't have enough trouble driving, it was sometimes all Roger could do to find his car. Parking lots were his worst nightmare, particularly at the Centrum Plaza in Kanata, near the Corel Centre, home of the Ottawa Senators, where he'd lose his car coming out of Denny's Restaurant.

"The guy who built this place should be shot," fumed Neilson, in uncharacteristically un-Christian fashion.

The combination of the Centrum lot and a rental car was too much for him altogether.

In his first season with Ottawa, Roger's Toyota truck was banged up in the Corel Centre parking lot and had to go in for repairs. He could not keep track of his replacement vehicle.

"What kind of car was it?" asked a reporter.

"A Sunbird or a Firebird or something," he said.

"That plaza over on Terry Fox Drive," he continued, referring to the dreaded Centrum Plaza, "is one of the most confusing in the world. Twice I've come out of there and gotten in the wrong car. I've had to say to people, 'Sorry, I have a red sports car, too.'"

The record shows that Neilson was losing cars long before he arrived in Ottawa. Devin Smith remembers Roger fumbling to get into a car, not his own, but convinced it was his because the keys worked. He started the car, noticed the ashtray was full of cigarette butts and said, "Somebody's been smoking in my car!"

Larry Pearson was driving with Roger on Highway 401 to Windsor. Neilson got sleepy – news bulletin – and handed the wheel over to young Pearson, who accidentally guided the truck into a construction lane of freshly paved highway. It was about a day before the laneway was scheduled to open. For miles they drove on the wrong side of the pylons, receiving stares and glares from astonished workers.

Neilson was with a group of kids in Montreal to see some hockey. He was driving back home to Toronto when he ran low on gas. Approaching Kingston, he had pulled off at an exit to fill up again when his car was rammed by another at an intersection. The front end of Neilson's car was wrecked, and Roger had to get back to teach school the next day.

He and his five companions crammed into a Kingston taxi to complete the two-hour drive to Toronto. The fare: $180.

Picture a grown man weeping.

Coach Wayne Cashman tells the story of Neilson, then with the Philadelphia Flyers, being directed to the airport one time, with a car to lead him and another car behind him. He still got lost.

HIS OWN BRAND OF PAR

Kent Pearce worked at a golf course and once had ideas of becoming a golf pro.

So, Kent, could Roger golf?

"At times, but not really. He had the worst swing in the world and yet sometimes he'd score fairly well. He'd hit a ball, it would go straight off, and he'd stand there and admire it and he'd try to figure out how he did it. Next time up, he'd put the club on his shoulder and think about it for about ten or fifteen seconds and he'd say, 'Forget about it.'"

One morning, Pearce, Roger, and Donnie Brooker were playing at Six Foot Bay in the Kawarthas. "Roger got up to tee off on the first hole and the ball just went straight in front of him," says Pearce. Donnie was sitting there with a coffee in his hand, and he just dumped it all over his midsection. You could never stand even directly beside Roger when he was golfing. You had to be at least five feet behind him, because there was no telling where the ball might go.

"He's the only person I've ever seen shank it completely straight, the other way."

For nearly twenty years, Roger made an annual summer pilgrimage to Hawaii. Sometimes he golfed. Usually, he was more interested in collecting golf balls, to extremes that the obsessive-compulsive would envy. Wealthy Americans and other tourists pay $145 green fees to play the spectacular courses of Kapalua.

And all Roger cared about was scooping errant Titleists. He was a ball hawk, not a ball striker.

"There were three courses there, and he had all the [ball-finding] holes picked out at each course," says Pearce. "In the final four years or so, we all had our own assignments. Our own holes to explore. The goal was to beat the total from the previous year.

"The Village number-nine hole was huge. This one par-five, dogleg right, has a huge ravine. Everyone slices, so there's tons of balls in there. I wasn't a big fan of collecting balls. I remember one time, sitting in the golf cart, waiting to go, all these people were passing us. Roger must have been down there for forty-five, fifty minutes, getting balls. He came up, his legs were bleeding, all cut, his shirt had clay all over it.

"He must have had 250 balls. He fell and was hanging by a branch over this cliff. Paul Mattucci, a member of our group, heard him and helped him up. Roger was nuts. Just loved collecting balls."

The grand haul: 1,700 balls, sorted and carted home to Canada in the group's luggage.

Dallas Eakins remembers when Neilson first discovered the ravine's secret hold of hundreds of golf balls. Down Roger went into the swampy mess, tossing up dozens of balls and shouting, "It's heaven down here."

On his final Hawaii trip, Roger was suffering from pneumonia. It didn't stop him from ball collecting.

Sometimes a Roger foursome in Hawaii didn't even pretend to need a golf bag. And scorecards were for ball tallies, not strokes.

Pearce says, "Late afternoon, he'd try to hustle everyone up – 'C'mon, we're going ball collecting' – and everyone would have a backpack and a bag, just filling them up. [Laughs uproariously.] Then we'd come back to the condo where we were staying, he'd get Javex and Tide and throw all the balls in the washing machine. To clean them up. And then he'd throw them in the dryer. Oh, man.

"He'd put them in the washer machine, and it was *loud*, then he'd close the door and he'd run, so no one would see that he was putting golf balls in there."

Shouldn't every condo come equipped with a ball-washing machine?

When Devin Smith was a rink rat, he used to golf with Roger on Wednesdays at 5:30 a.m.

Roger made certain that they'd get cart number 6, the cart with no speed regulator in it.

"We'd play a round of golf in an hour and fifteen minutes," says Smith. "I was fourteen or fifteen, flying down this hill, and I thought we were going to die. He wasn't being a yahoo about it, just driving along."

GILLIGAN'S "THREE-HOUR TOUR"

Roger loved to explore the Trent-Severn Waterway system. He would study the lock schedule to know what time he needed to leave to reach a particular destination in a day to access a certain lake or lock.

Everything was a game, a contest.

A declining gas gauge was just another challenge.

On a seventeen-foot bow rider with an eighty-five-horsepower engine, Neilson would try to negotiate the thirteen locks and 120 kilometres between Chemong Lake and Georgian Bay in a single day.

Occasionally, the skipper and his fearless crew would come close to drowning in Lake Simcoe.

A typical trip, this time involving Doug Jarvis, Dave Clements, and Al Dunford: after a rough Simcoe crossing, they docked the boat in Parry Sound. Next morning it was nowhere in sight. It had sunk. Water over the transom. Sleeping bags and some gear were completely soaked.

A huge forklift had to come and haul out the boat and motor, which could have used one of Roger's golf-ball dryers.

"We had to convince Jarvis to keep going," says Clements.

"He was scared to death, just wanted to get a taxi home."

Roger enjoyed taking his cottage guests tubing. Occasionally, he was in the tube.

On his worst day, he was alongside Kris King, a big, strong hockey player.

Devin Smith was driving the boat, fast enough, tight enough, to deliciously spill the contents of the tube – contents that smacked into each other as they crashed into the lake.

Several minutes later, after the boat had picked up Neilson and King, an Ontario Provincial Police cruiser happened by, inquiring about the boat's safety equipment.

Neilson had blood oozing out of a bump on his head. He was slightly disoriented.

"Do you have life jackets?"

"Oh yeah, I've got life jackets," mumbled Roger.

"Are you okay, sir?"

"Yeah, I'm fine, I'm fine."

"Do you have a bailer?"

"What's a bailer?" asked Neilson, the inveterate boater.

"Are you sure you're okay?"

Sometimes Roger lost the gasoline-calculation game. It happened on land and sea, once on a rather windswept day in rock-infested Georgian Bay.

His boat drifting helplessly, Captain Neilson ordered his crew, Todd Ervin and Darren Keily, to abandon ship before the vessel was smashed into kindling.

"Jump on the count of three," he shouted. "One! Two! Three!"

And of course Roger was the lone jumper, his teenage crew staying aboard, laughing at their little joke, as the boat thrashed perilously closer to rocks.

Now Roger was wet and furious.

"My boat's gonna smash! Get in, get in!"

Todd and Darren finally leaped, but it took Roger ages to cool down, despite the fresh water up to his neck.

They guided the boat ashore, where they could dry out and gas up and chalk up another adventure with Roger.

Roger wasn't big on using a wallet, especially in the lazy days of summer. He kept paper bills stuffed in the pockets of his shorts, and sometimes just sitting on the dashboard of his boat. While going through the lock at Bobcaygeon, his cash flew off the dash in a gust of wind, scattering over the water in the lock like leaves from a tree.

Roger wasn't much of a swimmer, but he dove into that lock water like Tarzan to retrieve his loot.

CLOTHES MAKE THE MAN

Roger despised wearing ties, but as an NHL coach he could not escape them.

So, Neilson did the next best thing to wearing no tie: he wore outrageous ones. He always credited (blamed?) Neil Smith of the New York Rangers as the inspiration behind the Neilson trademark tie – the louder and wilder the better.

Smith, the Rangers GM, would strut around with $175 neckties. As a form of protest at having to wear a tie and against Smith's vanity, Roger would seek out two- and three-dollar ties on the street, boast about his bargain, and claim to look as sharp as his boss.

As his fame grew, Roger didn't have to buy another tie. They were like golf balls from Hawaii. Friends and fans would see ties that made them think of Roger and send them to him by the carload.

He was forever giving them away.

When Devin Smith was living in Roger's house in Peterborough, Roger would call up after his Rangers games to compare notes. Smith was picking up the raw feed on satellite, so he could hear what Madison Square Garden broadcasters John Davidson and Sam Rosen were saying during commercials. During one break, J.D. and Rosen were panning Roger's choice of tie behind the bench. Over the phone, Smith told Roger he was getting grief about his tie, so Neilson wandered over to the broadcasters after the game and said, "I can't believe you're saying that about my tie."

Roger's standard outfit consisted of a ball cap, pair of shorts or track pants, a T-shirt, sandals or sneakers, and no socks.

It's how he was dressed when he met the president of Israel.

Roger was the easiest person on earth to get dressed, except that he could be fussy and unkempt at the same time.

In his late years he lived in an old russet-coloured Abercrombie & Fitch ball cap. One summer the hockey camp held a contest to find Roger a new hat. More than one hundred entries poured in, hats of all shapes, sizes, colours, and descriptions. Roger rejected each and every one.

Neilson's unique fashion sense didn't always mesh with the five-star attitude of the typical NHL hotel. One morning in Atlanta with the visiting Ottawa Senators, Neilson was on his way into the Ritz-Carlton hotel restaurant when he was instructed by the maître d' that it was closed. He directed Roger to a greasy spoon across the street. Later, Roger returned to the hotel to see several Senators players emerging from the hotel restaurant, which was obviously only "closed" to certain clientele.

"Hey," grumbled Roger to fellow assistant coach Perry Pearn, "I think that guy thought I was a bum!"

THE MAN'S BEST FRIEND

Particularly when he was younger, Roger felt more comfortable in the company of dogs than that of people.

"He would talk to them for hours, as a way of not having to talk to adults," says Paul Bedford. "He hated small talk. Didn't have any use for it. If he went to a function and a dog was there, it was a way to avoid talking. It was like an escape mechanism. He was very shy. He became a good speaker, but he worked at it."

Jacques was Roger's first great dog, a golden Lab–shepherd mix that Roger acquired when Jacques was about two years old. He lived to be eighteen. A pretty good run considering he lost a kidney at age six.

When Jacques died, in 1975, Roger said he cried for only the second time in his life.

"When it was obvious that Jacques was dying, Roger had the vet come to the cottage to give him the fatal needle rather than taking him to the vet," Dick Todd told *Canadian Magazine*. "He felt that Jacques would figure out he was going to be put away. Roger loved Jacques so much. At the end, when Jacques was very feeble, he even toyed with the idea of buying a supermarket buggy, putting a blanket in it, and pushing Jacques everywhere."

Jacques was buried on Neilson's cottage property at Buckhorn Lake, and when he sold that property, in 1985, he used to talk about digging up Jacques's grave and moving his remains to his home on Chemong Lake.

Roger made a plaque out of a wheelbarrow tray, with an inscription: "Here lies Jacques. 1958-1975. The Greatest Dog Ever."

Jacques's greatest contribution to the game of hockey was helping the Peterborough Petes understand the discipline and patience required to forecheck.

In what would become a classic tale in Roger lore, Roger brought Jacques onto the practice ice at the Memorial Centre and planted him in front of the net.

"Stay," he told his obedient pet.

Roger went behind the net with a puck, faked coming out one side, then out the other. Jacques stood as still as a statue.

Roger's forwards looked at Jacques a little sheepishly. The moral of the story was that if a dog had the patience to wait for the puck carrier to commit, a teenaged hockey player should, too.

"I don't think they liked the inference, but they got the message," said Neilson.

The other side of Jacques was that he was a natural hunter. And he didn't limit his blood lust to wild creatures. Once, when Roger's Peterborough baseball team was at a house barbecue, Jacques ate the family's pet hamster in the basement. Then, when Neilson scolded Jacques and shooed him outside, Jacques ate the family rabbit.

During a minor-league baseball game in Toronto, Jacques dragged a rabbit out to second base and ate it.

Dave Clements was among the youngsters who didn't share Roger's love of Jacques.

On a trip home from the ballpark, Clements was sitting beside Jacques in the back seat when the dog suddenly gagged and puked up a groundhog head.

"It looked like a hairball," says Clements.

"Jacques commanded the whole back seat." Clements continues. "Roger always drove a Ford Country Squire wagon in those days. The bigger, the better, because he had all the baseball equipment to carry and kids to transport.

"Jacques loved the back seat and he hated sitting in the back with the baseball equipment. Quite often, Jacques would

sit in the seat, and we'd sit back with the baseball equipment."

Roger's second great dog was Mike, a white mutt, part Labrador, that Al Dunford had come across among a litter of pups being given away just outside Peterborough. Al bought Mike as a gift for Roger, though Roger had to get to know him for a few days before agreeing on Mike as a replacement for Jacques.

Mike, it turns out, was just as adept as Jacques at hunting groundhogs.

When Roger took Mike golfing, which was always, Mike liked to bring back his kill to show off to Rog, or he'd haul it to the front steps of the golf course clubhouse and drop it on the steps.

It was a common scene, Mike lying beside a bloody ground-hog just outside the clubhouse.

Needless to say, Mike wasn't terribly popular on the Peterborough-area courses.

To say the least, Roger was an unconventional pet owner. His dogs wandered wherever they wanted. Usually, they found their way home. One evening in Buffalo, however, Mike was lost in the city. As head coach of the Sabres, Neilson had media connections, so he contacted a local radio station and got them to broadcast a description of Mike. Eventually, Roger and Dunford found Mike, not far from home, slightly lost but otherwise sound.

IS ANYBODY HOME?

Roger was breaking down game tape in New York when he called Devin Smith to chat about the game.

A prerequisite for being one of Roger's Boys, especially in his house, was to watch every game and be able to chat about it afterward.

Roger was on the phone with Smith, and every once in a while

he was grumbling to himself. "Crap," he said. "This remote doesn't work."

Smith, meanwhile, was trying to tell Roger about a particular essay he'd been working on for school, but could tell he didn't have Roger's attention on the line.

A few minutes later, Roger blurted out, "Oh, no."

"What's wrong?"

"I was trying to change the TV channel with a calculator."

Devin Smith was on the scene for the other legendary yarn involving Roger and appliances, in the mid-1980s.

While Roger was looking around inside a Peterborough electronics showroom, Smith was talking with a salesman.

"These TVs," complained Roger, "they're so small and so expensive."

"Roger," said Smith, "those are microwaves."

The gang ordered pizza at Roger's house.

It was a little cold, so Roger put it in the oven to warm it up, without thinking to take the pizza out of the box.

Minutes later, smoke was pouring out of the oven and Roger opened the door to see the pizza box on fire.

He put out the flames with a wet towel and laughed like a hyena at his mental gap.

"He thought it was the funniest thing he'd ever done," says Kent Pearce. "Roger was a brilliant man, but for a brilliant man he did some pretty weird and unexplainable things."

Roger dearly loved Nancy Nichols, his long-time companion, whom he met in Dallas in 1976.

But as recently as 1998, he was wrestling with the spelling of her last name.

He had a package to send to Nancy, and the Philadelphia Flyers beat writers were in his office.

"Does Bernie Nicholls spell his name with one *l* or two?" Neilson asked.

Told it was two, a reporter wondered, "Are you sending something to Bernie Nicholls?"

"No," said Roger. "I'm sending something to my friend. I can't remember how she spells her name, but I know it's the opposite of Bernie's."

Michael Farber told that one in *Sports Illustrated*.

Roger showed up at the Pearce household, hungry as usual.

Susan Pearce went into the kitchen to make him a sandwich and looked out the window. "Roger," she said, "is there someone in your car?"

"Oh my goodness," said Roger. "I forgot about [sister] Joanie."

Though meticulous with details, Roger was forever losing track of time. In arenas he could sit in the dining room telling stories and forget the game was about to start.

At an airport, trying to catch a flight home by himself, he was on the phone and looked up to see the gate closed. Adamant about catching his flight, he started banging on the glass, desperate now to get on.

The woman at the counter shook her head and pointed to her watch. Neilson continued to pound the glass, causing a scene.

"I've *got* to catch this flight," he said.

"Sir, look around," said the woman.

Roger looked around and saw a hundred people waiting to get on the same flight, now all staring at him. The gate hadn't opened yet.

When he became head coach in Philadelphia in 1997, Neilson got lost so often walking between the coaches' offices and the players' bench at the First Union Center (now Wachovia Center) that a staffer, for a gag, ran a string along the corridor and through the various doorways. Instead of being insulted, Roger was disappointed when the guideline was removed. "None of the stinkin' doors have names on them, so the string makes sense," said Neilson.

Dean Brown and Greg Millen were broadcasting a Senators game in Raleigh, North Carolina, during the 2001-02 season when they gazed down from the press box at a remarkable pre-game scene. Seems that Roger, already running late, had been stopped on his way to the players' bench by a security guard who wanted to chat. Roger chatted with everyone. As a result, he was late and lost. By the time he found the entranceway to cross the ice to the bench, the Canadian anthem had started and Roger was frozen against the boards, just beyond the spotlight shining on Carolina goaltender Arturs Irbe. Sheepish but respectful, Roger stood there, a few feet from Irbe, through both anthems before he could get to the bench.

CHEAP, CHEAP

Friends of Roger's tell tales of the hockey camp director driving around Lindsay or Peterborough to find the cheapest ping-pong balls in town. A dollar wasn't too insignificant a saving.

When he died, Roger left some old savings bonds worth $300,000 sitting in old cardboard box. He had apparently forgotten about them.

Staff playbooks, containing drills and activities, used to come into the camp on European-size paper, so it would get jammed when the staff tried to run it off on the camp photocopier.

Staff took the material up to a printer and had enough copies done to fill fifty books. Roger went ballistic when he saw the bill for $110.

This was the same man who thought nothing of spending $30,000 or $40,000 to take a group of youngsters to Australia, New Zealand, and Africa.

Postage was always a major issue with Roger, who was constantly firing off a bulk mailing someplace, for his coaches' clinic, or the hockey camp. His Christmas mailing list was larger than his *Globe and Mail* route.

Using a delivery service cost money, which meant it was a waste of resources by Roger's way of thinking.

So, he'd slap on a forty-eight-cent stamp, or whatever the going rate was, and whatever the weight of the envelope, and hope for the best. Sometimes they came right back at him from the Bridgenorth Post Office with a note about "insufficient postage."

"Crap," he'd say.

And he had a plan.

"You know what?" he said to a couple of his camp assistants. "What if you buy a coffee and donut and take it down to the lady at the Ennismore P.O.? She might let them through."

"So we take them down, these eight hundred letters, boxes of them," says Bedford. "And we give the lady the donut and coffee and we left her there with the boxes.

"We come back and tell Rog, and he's just smiling away, so happy he got all these letters through and saved twenty cents a letter."

Two hours later, the woman called and said, "I'm sorry, but these letters are all overweight. You've got to come back and pay to put larger stamps on them."

They went back and paid the extra postage without telling Roger the bad news. It would have killed him.

Don Liesemer, inspired by Roger to form Hockey Ministries International, tells a classic story about Roger trying to save a few dollars with his massive annual Christmas mailing.

The Neilson Christmas card industry had its origins in the late 1980s when Neilson was asked by a minister presiding over a men's Bible study group to write a personal note on the meaning of Christmas. Roger shared the message with a few friends, and eventually his yuletide list grew beyond one thousand.

In 1997, when Roger was an assistant coach with the St. Louis Blues, he asked Liesemer to meet him at the Molson Centre (now Bell Centre) after practice. When he arrived Liesemer was confronted with two giant goaltender bags and four boxes, all filled with Christmas mail and presents. Neilson had brought the cargo across the border with the team's hockey equipment – to skip having to pay American postage.

"After dragging the boxes and bags over snowbanks and streets into this crowded little post office in Montreal, packed with impatient Christmas mailers . . . if you can just picture the reaction of the other customers. It was disbelief. Everyone was looking at us. We had this huge cargo, and the others had an envelope or two. What could these two men be thinking?

"We shuffled our cargo inch by inch and finally got to the front of the line. And now, picture Roger at the counter, meticulously organizing the postage for each package and negotiating as well. He was totally unmoved by the boos and heckling of that large crowd behind him, who probably had no idea who he was."

Roger made the most of the few days that hockey professionals get to spend with their families at Christmas. Roger's Christmas

"family" included sister Joan, until she died in 1998, and the Bells, Pearces, and Mac Brick.

The tradition was to enjoy Christmas Eve at the Bricks' farm house on Chemong Lake. On Christmas Day, the gang moved down the street to Roger's.

Susan Pearce would cook the turkey dinner and cater to the invasion.

At Roger's insistence, presents were to be opened at 11 a.m. Sharp.

"I did a stocking for him every year, and he was like a big kid," says Susan. "He couldn't wait to see it. He'd look for it, and if he couldn't find it, he'd say, 'Isn't there a stocking for me?'

"I wrapped all the gifts inside the stocking and he tried to guess what they were, but he couldn't ever guess.

"I used to include a [Don Cherry] *Rock 'Em, Sock 'Em* video, and one year I didn't have one in there and he was so disappointed."

When Roger was out to dinner with friends following his initial diagnosis for multiple myeloma, the restaurateur, knowing Roger and the news, insisted the meal was on the house.

"Hey," mumbled Roger to his table guests, "this cancer thing isn't half bad!"

Life on the East Coast

H e was Roger's most reliable "winger," a tireless digger who happened to be the coach's best friend.

Mike, a stocky white part-Labrador with a taste for fresh groundhog meat, also had something many of Roger's players envied. Freedom.

Neilson always let his dogs run free. It was his players he kept on short leashes. In New York City, while he was working for an organization he loved, hired by a bright, young GM named Neil Smith, and living in oceanside digs he cherished, Neilson's tight control and obsession with defensive hockey would cost him his job – or at least the combination of his coaching style and having Mark Messier as his captain would cost him his job.

And it may have cost him a Stanley Cup.

We can't know, because the Rangers went ahead and won without him. Roger Neilson's NHL coaching career is usually

described in glowing terms related to his creative influence on hockey and his caring relationships with people in the game. Neilson worked around the clock on behalf of his team and for the betterment of the game. He had an uncommon personal interest in players and their families. These are fundamental issues in any assessment of the man; they are what separate him from the coaching pack.

Still, the pack also concerns itself with champagne-soaked championships and springtime skates around the rink with the precious Stanley Cup. On this particular scorecard, Roger's 1,000-game career as a head coach is marked by close calls and many not so close, by ill-timed dismissals, and by teams that, to Neilson's detriment, overachieved on his watch. Only once was Neilson involved with a Cup-winning program, and his role was so minor – a temporary analyst breaking down video during the playoff run of the 1984 Edmonton Oilers, while living in a hotel room across from the arena – that he wasn't associated with the championship. Captain Video was strictly a home-movie specialist in that series; he didn't accompany the Oilers on the road.

For Neilson to take on that inglorious part-time job was proof, if it were needed, that his love of work was greater than his sense of ego. That he would create his legend without winning a Cup says much about the impact he had on the game and the close hockey family within it. A glance at Neilson's lineups over the years reveals a general pattern and this clear consideration: nobody handed him the keys to the Montreal Canadiens, the New York Islanders, or the Oilers, the three dynasties that roamed the NHL during Neilson's tenure.

Typically, Neilson directed ordinary, hard-working teams that reflected the honest ethic of their coach. During his fifteen seasons as a head coach, in whole or partial seasons, he was the patron saint of the checking forward. He gave us Bob Gainey, Doug Jarvis, and Craig Ramsay, three of the most relentless – and in the

case of Jarvis, most durable – checkers in the history of the game. He did it by wiring their pliable young minds in junior. If they were to rename the Selke Trophy, awarded annually to the top defensive forward, it should be the Neilson Trophy or perhaps, in honour of the prototype, they should name it after Gainey himself.

It was Neilson, remember, who once said, as the coach of the Toronto Maple Leafs in the late 1970s, "I'd probably be happiest trying to win a Cup with twenty-five Jimmy Joneses."

A former Peterborough Pete under Neilson, Jones played two full NHL seasons, both with Roger's Leaf teams from 1977 to 1979, and scored thirteen goals in the league. His career waned after Neilson left the organization.

Neilson gave life to players who might not otherwise have played in the game's best league, and for that they're eternally grateful. He doled out ice time to third- and fourth-line players, and made them feel important. Had he been able to do that and get along with Messier at the same time, Neilson might have been riding in the 1994 Stanley Cup parade in New York City. He wasn't. Neilson lost Messier, then his coaching job, in mid-season of 1992-93. Months later, good friend and fellow Petes alumnus Mike Keenan, with Messier fully onside, stepped in and fired up the Rangers to their first Cup victory in fifty-four years. Thanks for setting the table, Rog.

Neilson coached some other skilled players through the years besides Messier, and got along with most of them considerably better, once they got over raising eyebrows at his antics. Eric Lindros, Mike Gartner, Brian Leetch, Adam Graves, Bernie Nicholls, John LeClair, Mark Recchi, Thomas Gradin, Gilbert Perreault, Darryl Sittler, Borje Salming, and Lanny McDonald were some of the stars who, for the most part, raved about Neilson as a head coach.

He directed a few contending teams, but not many. Neilson's best teams were probably the 1977-78 Leafs, who lost out to the

Canadiens in the Cup semifinals; the 1991-92 Rangers, who won 50 games; and the 1999-2000 Flyers, who fell in the Cup semifinals under Craig Ramsay's direction after Neilson was diagnosed with cancer. The 1981-82 Vancouver Canucks played over their heads to reach the Cup finals.

A more typical Neilson scenario saw him instruct and prepare a team for great things, then get canned and watch someone else get the glory. The Rangers were the best example. Neilson taught them how to check and play disciplined hockey, lessons that didn't entirely leave them when they opened up their game under Keenan.

During his tenure in Florida, which rivals the Vancouver run as his finest coaching achievement, Neilson took an expansion team and had it playing .500 hockey when new management stepped in and fired him after the second season. The next year, the Panthers were in the Cup finals.

As cruel as any firing must be, nobody in the game was fired as often and as cruelly as Neilson. Neilson was, in the words of the *Ottawa Citizen,* "the doer of many good deeds and seemingly none of them go unpunished."

Joe Lapointe covered the Rangers for the *New York Times.* When asked about Roger, Lapointe pays him this unusual compliment: "He was very good at being fired. By that I mean, he always took it with grace. He didn't get mad at anybody or burn any bridges."

Considering the circumstances of his firings, Neilson had cause to be angry, spiteful, vengeful. The Bible taught him to forgive, to turn the other cheek and love his enemies. Boy, did he get practice at it.

Flash summations of his time off for good behaviour:

1. Toronto Maple Leafs: He's a victim of Ballard the Buffoon, who fires Neilson twice without telling him once.

2. Buffalo Sabres: Less about team performance and more about a clash of personalities between Neilson and Scotty Bowman.

3. Vancouver Canucks: Neilson takes a middling team on a mind-altering ride to the Cup finals and pays for the hangover.

4. Los Angeles Kings: Neilson has bigger plans than this twenty-eight-game mop-up job.

5. New York Rangers: Messier plays Brutus; Neilson, Caesar. You get the picture.

6. Florida Panthers: Neilson sparks expansion club, he's in his teaching element, but a new principal arrives.

7. Philadelphia Flyers: Roger gets cancer and deals with it better than the Flyers organization, which tactlessly replaces him.

There's a certain frustration associated with Neilson's coaching career. It's as though the wanderlust in his life away from the game spilled over into it, no matter how much he craved stability in the workplace. Considering he was just the ninth member of the NHL coach's 1,000-game club – think Al Arbour, Scotty Bowman, Dick Irvin, Sr., Billy Reay – Neilson didn't really get to sink his teeth into a single lasting coaching situation, unlike those proto-types of coaching longevity. The closest he came to a steady job was in New York, his longest stopover – precisely three and a half seasons, 280 games.

To use a baseball analogy, which Neilson would favour, he was a relief pitcher called in from the bullpen to settle situations. Not a closer. That sort of work went to people like Keenan, brought in to push a close team over the top with his emotional fire and will. Roger, determined but soft-spoken, was more of a middle-inning guy by reputation, the selfless reliever who often heroically keeps a team in a ball game to provide the glory guy with the chance to close it out. Middle relievers aren't on the field when the celebrating starts. And it takes some reflection to appreciate their subtle but vital role after the fact.

Neilson inherited a bit of a mess when he arrived in Manhattan in 1989 to coach the Rangers, but he also had a core of talent with which to work. And through additions made by general manager Neil Smith, that talent base grew after he got there.

Neilson's career win-loss record stands up to scrutiny: 460 victories, 381 losses, 159 ties, despite employment with a raw expansion club in Florida and a Vancouver team possessed more of guile than skill. Having losing teams didn't send Neilson packing – with the possible exception of Vancouver – it was the environmental issues within each organization. The coach's worst enemies: circumstances, timing, personalities, and, to borrow his favourite adjective, crappy luck. This was especially evident in his final three stops as a head coach – New York, Florida, and Philadelphia.

It may surprise some, in retrospect, to learn that Neilson left the Rangers having recorded the second-highest winning percentage in franchise history among coaches whose tenure exceeded one season. With Roger's record of 141-104-35, or a .566 victory percentage, only Emile "The Cat" Francis, with a .602 percentage in three stints from 1965 to 1975, had better numbers.

Of course, in the Cat's day players knew their place, which was usually under the thumb of an owner or his hired managers. In Manhattan of 1992, a revered millionaire centre like Mark Messier, laden as he was with five Stanley Cup rings from his Edmonton Oilers days and gunning for a sixth, had both the aura and the clout to get a coach fired if he so desired.

For a while, it looked as though Messier and Neilson were going to make beautiful music together. Acquired by GM Smith in a multi-player deal that saw Bernie Nicholls go to Edmonton, Messier was welcomed as the great saviour in New York, a leader of mystical proportions who could will his teammates to victory with a single glare, or so was his reputation. New York, which only has time for the biggest stars, went nuts for Messier. And

Neilson was as thrilled as anyone to have Mess on board. "When a player of his stature stands up, players listen," he told reporters.

In his first season with the Rangers, Messier was sixth in league scoring, with Oiler-esque type numbers: 35 goals, 72 assists, 107 points. He had other reasons to be pleased. Adam Graves, Messier's loyal Oilers pal, was rock solid on the wing and building up to his best NHL seasons. Young defenceman Brian Leetch was becoming an offensive star. Tony Amonte was the top scorer among rookies and, as always, Neilson had a strong cast of grinders like Kris King, Jeff Beukeboom, and Tie Domi.

Messier had just the kind of dressing-room impact that Smith and Neilson hoped he would. As Jeff Klein reminds us in *Messier,* the 2003 biography of the legendary centre, one of his first acts was to remove a large table from the middle of the Rangers room. Cluttered as it usually was with water coolers, cups, tape, and so on, the table kept players from being able to see certain other players. The new captain wanted to be able to look each and every player in the eye. Routinely, he called players-only meetings and spoke passionately about his lack of tolerance for subpar effort from anyone, himself included.

Quietly, after just a couple of months in the uniform, Messier was already grumbling to GM Smith about Neilson's coaching style. As he had in Toronto, Buffalo, and Vancouver, Neilson had turned the Rangers into a respectable team with a focus on defensive responsibility; in other words, the polar opposite of the freewheeling firewagon hockey played by Messier, Wayne Gretzky, Jari Kurri, and the rest of the dynastic Oilers of the 1980s. Neilson was a hockey conservative and stood out in these years by plugging up the neutral zone with checkers, not yet a staple of every team's system.

He had a case to take to court. Roger got results. In a single season under Neilson, the year before Messier's arrival from Edmonton, the Rangers reduced their goals-against by forty. That

they also scored about thirty fewer goals didn't prevent them from winning the Patrick Division with 85 points in 1989-90, ending a seven-year run in which the Rangers had never finished higher than third in their division.

In some NHL towns, winning a division is a ho-hum deal compared to what really matters, playoff success. But in New York, which hadn't won a division title since the Second World War, it was enough to diminish, if not entirely halt, the chants of "Nineteen-forty!" that rang out from the stands, home and away, as a derisive reference to the Rangers' last Stanley Cup–winning season.

Kris King, one of Roger's hockey school disciples, followed Neilson to New York. When Neilson was hired by Smith as head coach, King's father told Kris, "I bet Roger is going to trade for you." Days later, Smith did just that on Neilson's behalf.

King remembers the shocked reaction of the Rangers' top scorers to Neilson's strategy. "He brought the trap to a team that had John Ogrodnick, Brian Mullen, and Bernie Nicholls," says King. "The guys kind of looked at him. All of a sudden we win the Presidents' Trophy, first overall in the NHL. They bought into it. I remember Chris Nilan saying, 'We can't play this.' The first game, we give up one goal and eighteen shots on net, and Nilan says, 'Hey, this stuff works.' He made believers out of people."

By the time the Rangers finished first overall in 1991-92, Nicholls was gone and Messier was the man.

According to King, Neilson's modus operandi was first to convince his worker bees, the third- and fourth-line forwards and fourth, fifth, and sixth defencemen, to believe in his systems play. Once they were onside, the more-skilled players could see the benefits and join in.

"It only worked if everybody did it," says King. "It was a five-man skating system, and if there was a breakdown somewhere, it left gaping holes. But if everybody did his job and trusted that everyone else would do his, it was a pretty effective system. And for a

while there in New York, it was as good as anywhere in the league."

Even Messier wasn't immune from catching heck on Roger's cursed videos. As King says – lovingly, of course – "It got so you didn't want to be on that damn videotape."

One time, Neilson pointed out a Messier mistake during a team video session. "It was like, 'Oh, my God, what's he doing?'" says King. "You just don't cross Messier.

"Then when we go back out on the ice, guys are skating around in practice, and thinking, 'Holy Christ, what was that?' Then, Roger goes over and talks to him. And we're thinking, 'Oh, man, he's giving it to him again!'"

Roger confided to King later that he was telling Messier, "Look, I appreciate you allowing me to use you to make a point to the rest of the guys. That's what a good captain does, and I appreciate it."

That didn't likely placate the captain, but it certainly sent an old-school message to the rest of the team. Says King, "Here's nineteen other guys looking at him and thinking, 'This guy's nuts. Taking on Mess?' We never knew what he said to him, but we figured he's just giving it to him. So it's like, it's not just us fourth-liners that are accountable, it's everybody."

With Messier, everything seemed possible. The most jaded of Rangers fans imagined an end to a fifty-year wait for glory. In a schedule reduced by four games, Roger's Rangers finished first overall in the NHL with 105 points, with no other team reaching triple figures.

Nicely spoiled by his Oilers successes, Messier made a point of accepting the Presidents' Trophy and setting it aside. The message being, the Moose was after bigger game.

Kris King still believes it could have happened that season. In the division final, the Rangers were leading the Pittsburgh Penguins by two goals in the third period of game four. After King performed a nifty imitation of a scoring star, getting the game-winning goals in

games two and three, the latter in overtime, the Rangers just had to hang on to take a 3-1 series lead back to New York for game five. Despite missing Mario Lemieux due to a broken hand suffered in game two, the Penguins scored two short-handed goals, one on a weak wrister by Ron Francis, to send game four into overtime. They won it, and eventually took the series in six games. The Penguins didn't lose another playoff game that spring, sweeping Boston and Chicago to win their second straight Stanley Cup.

Despite a watershed season, the Rangers could only look ahead to next year. As usual.

"This team is going to win a Stanley Cup," Messier told reporters after the loss to Pittsburgh. What he didn't say, but believed in his heart, was that they would do it without Neilson as head coach.

It escaped no one's notice when Messier stood up at the awards dinner in the summer of 1992 to accept his Hart Trophy as league MVP and thanked seemingly everyone in the Rangers organization, down to the arena caretakers, except Neilson, who sat in the audience as a candidate for coach-of-the-year honours.

The lively New York press had a field day with the simmering feud between the coach and his brightest star. While Neil Smith, a Roger supporter, was working behind the scenes to try to mend the damage, Messier was providing damning quotes to eager reporters. Specifically, he spoke of being weary of Neilson's weak forecheck system: lying back in wait for an offensive force like the Penguins to get into the neutral zone. "When you've got a team that can skate like ours," he said, "you want to apply pressure all over the ice."

Messier may have earned a reputation as a coach killer, but Neilson was not going to change his coaching style for any player, even Messier. Their differences stewed all summer after the NHL awards snub. Neilson knew he was in trouble.

He confided to those closest to him. Defenceman Dallas Eakins, a regular pro visitor to Roger's hockey camp, remembers golfing with Neilson at 6:00 a.m. one day that summer. Roger told Eakins, "If I can't fix things with Messier, I'm going to get fired."

Eakins later played with Messier on the Rangers. He knew both men, respected both, the great leader and the coach without enemies. "For those two not to get along, it amazed me," says Eakins.

In Frank Brown's book *Broadway Blues,* Colin Campbell, a Rangers assistant coach at the time, compared Neilson and Messier to a couple bound for divorce. "There was that tension between them and it made you feel uneasy," said Campbell, now the NHL's executive vice-president. "They wouldn't say anything, but you knew there was something wrong; you just wished they'd be back together again."

Smith played marriage counsellor, a futile role he didn't relish. "There's really nothing I could have done," he would say months later. "I have a lot of respect for both of them, but I don't think I could have changed the situation."

Like many a troubled couple, they attempted a reconciliation. As the team gathered for training camp in the fall of 1992, Messier and Neilson huddled for a lengthy meeting. The proverbial white smoke rose from the chimney, and both men emerged to profess mutual respect.

"I think we can work with each other," said Messier.

"All's well," said Roger, that ends, uh, badly.

After a strong start by the team, Neilson was awarded a three-year contract extension at $275,000 per season. But now injuries became an issue, including Messier's bad back, and the Rangers hit a slump. Messier made critical remarks in the press about what he viewed as excessive player movement, lineup changes, and chemistry issues in the room.

Remember when Neilson used to meet with several player lieutenants from the Maple Leafs dressing room? Well, he tried

the same thing in New York. Unbelievably, Messier was not among the players he consulted to discuss some of the team issues. Behind the captain's back, Neilson met with such loyal Messier allies as Adam Graves, Kevin Lowe, and Mike Gartner. The coach felt that Messier was sulking and that if these secondary leaders could show the way, the captain just might be shamed into coming back to life.

It was a fatal move. The Rangers were on their way to missing the playoffs, and they would do it without Neilson. He was fired after forty games, proving that the Moose is mightier than the fresh contract extension.

Smith, a young GM who admired and respected Roger, told the *New York Daily News* that he was "devastated" at having to fire Neilson. "I could hardly pick my head up to tell him," said Smith. "I hated myself for it."

Now fully branded a coach killer, Messier didn't feel much better. The rest of the season was a disaster. Brian Leetch, New York's brilliant defenceman, broke his ankle in a late-night escapade with Messier. All the hopes raised by the previous Presidents' Trophy season were in tatters, and as related in Klein's biography, Messier told reporters, while the players performed the annual season-end ritual of cleaning out their locker stalls, "Right now I don't feel like playing another game in my entire life. My mind's about ready to explode."

He also said he didn't want to end his New York career on such a sour note.

As history would show, he didn't. Messier and Neilson would both rise again.

It took Roger a while to recover from what he saw as a player acting out of turn. Scheduled to meet hockey broadcaster Dick Irvin to talk about coaching for Irvin's book, Neilson unloaded on Messier, for the record.

"A guy like Messier is brought in to win a Stanley Cup," Neilson told Irvin, in *Behind the Bench* days after the firing. "He's paid a very large salary and there is a lot of pressure on him. He plays a year and they don't quite do it. Now he's looking for reasons and he decides that we're not going to win with this coach. So he goes to management and tells them they're just not going to win with this guy. He says because he is the leader of the team it's his job to make that known.

"Some media people said that was right. Well, I think it's entirely wrong. A player is brought in to play and show leadership on the ice. If you have a player stepping into management I think you've got a chaotic situation. I think the player will lose his relationship with the players on the team because all of a sudden he's making the decisions on who is going to be the coach and who is going to be on the team. However, with the huge salaries being paid out, I think you're going to see more and more of that happening. All of a sudden these days young guys in their mid-twenties read that they're making three times as much as the President of the United States and I think it affects some of them.

"Ten years ago, if a player had ever walked up to Jim Gregory or Scotty Bowman, or whoever was my general manager, and said, 'Listen, this coach has got to go,' any one of those guys would have told him so fast to get lost and then would have told him to get back on the ice and start playing. But today, it's a different story.

"I've been with a lot of teams but nothing like this has come close to happening before. It's too bad because the experience in New York was the best of my career. I loved it there. I really loved the team. It has some great character guys. Our practice rink was out in Rye and everybody lives about five minutes from the rink. Sunday was always kind of an optional-skate deal and the guys would bring their kids. We had a big basket of candies in the office and the kids would all come in. It's the only

team where I got to know a lot of the wives and kids, and it was a great feeling. There was a real family atmosphere and good hardworking team. I never had that feeling with any other team. To leave there was really tough."

It got tougher a couple of days later when Roger's beloved dog, Mike, died. With tears running down his face, Roger carried him out of the animal hospital in a cardboard box and carted him across the border to be buried on his property near Peterborough.

"He went everywhere with me," Neilson told Irvin. "He was never tied up, just wandered freely around Buffalo and Chicago, everywhere I went. I don't know how he survived all those places. He was an unbelievable dog. I could tell you a million stories about him. I had people phoning me from all over Canada and the United States, more about Mike dying, really, than about my dismissal. He made quite a name for himself."

Neilson's former assistant Ron Smith, who was coaching the Rangers farm team in Binghamton, New York, took over for the rest of the 1992-93 season before Keenan was hired.

Typically, Neilson made it easier for Smith to step in.

"It was awkward," says Smith. "But he wrote the nicest, most encouraging letter to me you could imagine. Told me he knew I could handle it. It was bittersweet."

Even more so one year later when Smith was back in Vancouver as an assistant to Pat Quinn and the Canucks lost game seven to Keenan's Rangers in the Stanley Cup finals.

A SUNNY INTERLUDE

By the time Roger checked in to Sunrise, Florida, in 1993 as the first head coach of the expansion Florida Panthers, he was entering the twilight of his coaching career. And he had never felt better.

This hardy Canadian boy raised on Foster Hewitt broadcasts and all things Maple Leaf lapped up the new flavour of hockey in the American Sunbelt. If Neilson told Dick Irvin that coaching

New York was his best NHL experience, he changed his mind after he ventured a few hundred miles to the south along the Atlantic Ocean. South Florida's relaxed outdoor lifestyle, combined with the excitement of building an organization from the ground up, made this a blessed hockey destination in Roger's eyes. The man rarely wore socks in Canadian winter, after all, so imagine the intoxication of feeling the warm sand running between those callused toes.

"You have to remember, Roger was a beach bum," says Dallas Eakins, a defenceman on Neilson's Panthers team. "He could walk down the steps and out his back door and he was on the beach. He would sit and have his morning coffee and read the Bible, then jump on his mountain bike and ride to work, wearing his grubby shorts and flip-flops. Nothing could be better. And when he got to the rink, there was a group of guys ready to work hard. There were no problems."

Brought into the NHL just a year after the Tampa Bay Lightning, the Panthers were going to be the cousin down the street, though not the poor cousin, it turned out, that the Lightning had envisioned.

Hired eleven days before his fifty-ninth birthday, Neilson was the ideal coach for the collection of veteran castoffs and young prospects that would make a surprisingly slick entry into the league.

When Neilson came on board, Bobby Clarke had already been the club's general manager for three months. Bill Torrey, who had helped create the New York Islanders dynasty, was hired as president under the ownership of Blockbuster Video mogul H. Wayne Huizenga. A formidable group. And it could not have enjoyed better timing.

Having learned a lesson from the punishing expansion-draft formula that made instant jokes out of the Lightning and Ottawa Senators in 1992, the NHL served up a much-improved player pool for Clarke and Neilson with their start-up operation a year later. It

took Ottawa and Tampa Bay years before their annual high draft picks paid off in franchise success – the Senators were especially prudent in keeping their prospects – and the Lightning won the race to the Cup in 2004. The Panthers, meanwhile, were in the game from the beginning.

In the expansion draft, Clarke and his management team drafted such useful players as goaltender John Vanbiesbrouck, Scott Mellanby, Tom Fitzgerald, Brian Skrudland (the first captain), Andrei Lomakin, Dave Lowry, Joe Cirella, and Bill Lindsay. Centre Rob Niedermayer was their first pick in the entry draft. Stu Barnes, Bob Kudelski, Jody Hull, Keith Brown, and Brian Benning were acquired through trade or free agency. Vanbiesbrouck – whose rights were won by the Panthers with a coin toss against the other expansion franchise, Anaheim – was brilliant in Florida, instantly the most attractive player in a new hockey market.

On different nights, different players stepped up to carry this remarkable collection of retreads. These were Neilson's kind of players. Rugged, responsible, and, for the most part, veterans. With no top line, Neilson had no stars who needed coddling.

Winning about as often as they lost, the Panthers were the most successful first-year club of the NHL's expansion era. While their 33-34-17 record more or less matched the start-up perform-ance of the 1967 Philadelphia Flyers, the longer schedule of the 1990s helped the Panthers become the first expansion team to break 80 points, with 83. They exceeded all expectations. Neilson was there to set the defensive recipe, as always, but also to stir the pot as required. He appealed to his players' sense of pride, playing up the fact that many of them were left unprotected by their former organizations. Didn't they want to show the bastards they were wrong?

"We all loved being there," says Eakins. "Everyone really bought into Roger's philosophy of 'let's do something special here.'"

With success, the boys didn't even seem to mind playing a dull brand of hockey. *Sports Illustrated* told the story of Lowry jumping up in the dressing room before a nationally televised game against the Canadiens to declare, "All right, you guys, let's get out there and . . . put Canada to sleep!"

Evidently, the Canadiens, defending Stanley Cup champions at the time, snoozed along with the country, losing that game 8-3 and dropping another game 3-1 to Florida that season. The losses led the Habs coach of the day, Jacques Demers, to declare, "The Panthers are for real."

They were having a ball, most of all their head coach, happily working alongside a couple of his former players and now coaching understudies Craig Ramsay and Lindy Ruff.

"It was a great experience," says Ramsay, now a Cup champion as an assistant coach on the Lightning staff. "It was a brand-new team and the coaches were involved right from the beginning, picking players. We had a system and good leaders. Guys like Skrudland, Gord Murphy, Cirella, Keith Brown. They worked their butts off. It was pretty exciting. We were more of a pressure team than people knew. We were a hard team to play against. They all hated us, because we weren't supposed to win. We could skate. We forechecked and chased more than we trapped."

After fifteen years in the NHL, Neilson could appreciate having a good bunch of guys in the dressing room. Overall, this may have been his favourite group. He would join them for dinner. They'd hang around his office like rink rats. The seaside hockey scene was a huge novelty for players and fans. The Panthers' media guide depicted a player skating on the beach at low tide. This was one big, happy Southern family. And a nice place to visit for the woman in Roger's life.

"Florida was the best time in both of our lives," says Nancy Nichols. "Roger was so happy. He was much more relaxed. He brought his boat down. He loved that team. Had a great place on

the beach, which I wish he'd never sold. He wished he'd never sold, too. It was on Deerfield Beach, about twenty steps from the Boca Raton border. A twenty-minute bike ride to the Panthers practice rink in Fort Lauderdale.

"The organization was great," says Nichols. "It was Bobby Clarke at his finest. I gotta tell you, Bobby Clarke was a different person in Florida. And Bill Torrey. They did a lot of fun things; they had money at that time with Huizenga. They used to have team parties where they'd rent a big yacht and go out and have fun. The team was going great, it was a new hockey city, and everybody was on fire."

The same could be said of Nancy's relationship with Roger. Florida was one of the three times during a twenty-five-year, on-and-off romance that Nancy and Roger "almost" got married. The other two were during his later battles with cancer. Before Nancy, Roger had two semi-serious relationships. He dated a teacher named Mary in Peterborough and, while with Buffalo and Vancouver, quietly spent time with a woman from St. Catharines – Jill. Harry Neale can still remember Roger's flushed face when Jill came chasing after Neilson as he boarded a team bus one time – she was bringing him his forgotten jacket.

Nancy did get married, to a rock promoter in Los Angeles. After eight years, in 1992, the marriage ended in divorce. Nancy then moved back to Dallas, where she remains today, writing and editing food and travel articles for *D Magazine*. In her working career, along with the promotional work with the Chicago Blackhawks, Nancy has been a general manager with the Dallas Diamonds – a women's professional basketball team – and an event coordinator for the L.A. Coliseum and Sports Arena. She also operated her own event management company in Los Angeles.

"We talked about getting married so many times. He just wanted to keep going the way he was going. I don't have any regrets about that. We probably would have hated each other had we gotten

married. It doesn't change the fact I never loved anybody the way I loved him."

Southern Florida was a short flight from Texas, a flight that Nancy took frequently. She didn't want to miss out on the carnival that was the early Panthers. Disney World minus the commercialism.

Veteran Keith Brown, who came over from Chicago to solidify the Panthers defence, wrote a testimonial letter to Neilson years later about the Florida experience: "I distinctly remember having dinner with my wife and saying I had forgotten how much fun it was to play hockey."

Neilson docked his boat next to the home rented by Bill Lindsay and Rob Niedermayer, on the Intercoastal Waterway. Sometimes he'd call them up and tell them to bring it around, anchor it in front of his place on the ocean. One time he told the boys to drop it in front of his house because he was going out to dinner up the coast. So, Roger swam out to the anchored boat and attracted so many ocean lice inside his trunks, they were still with him when he showered at the rink the next day.

Another day, another Roger adventure. Like the time he was levelled by a car while cycling to the rink for the morning game-day skate. Ramsay, Neilson's assistant, tells the story.

"I came in early, thought I might even beat him into work for once, but when I get there he's sitting at his desk, with his arm up and a big ice pack on it. He says, 'A guy ran a *green* light.'

"At 6:00 a.m., I guess Roger figured no one was on the roads. So he had his head down and rode right through a red light. A car smacked him and he flew off his bike and landed on his arm. He had a fractured elbow, but the worse pain was in his wrist. It was a bad sprain. He did the morning meeting, then went off to the hospital to get it looked at. He came back and had a big cast on his arm, up over his elbow. He pulled a track suit on and coached the game that night. Next day, they took the cast off and put his arm in a sling. I guess they told him that if he kept the cast on, he

wouldn't be able to use the elbow properly again. So the cast came off and he just kept on going."

Other than Neilson mishaps, everything the Panthers touched that first season turned as gold as the cat on the gaudy team jerseys. They owned the mighty Canadiens, home and away. Vanbiesbrouck and Bob Kudelski ventured off to the All-Star Game in New York and Kudelski scored a pair of goals.

Away from the rink, Roger was closer to these particular players than he was with any other organization. The Panthers were one of two NHL teams that held a training camp in Peterborough, with side trips to Roger's home on Chemong Lake.

"We must have had a hundred people at his house," says Nancy. "He was so excited to have everybody come to Peterborough. He wanted to have camp up there all the time, because he wanted everyone at his place. The Panthers did it and the Flyers did it. For the Panthers, we did a big steak dinner. It was me and Mary Todd and some of the neighbours. We cooked for a hundred guys. And I finally got Roger to allow beer at his house. I said, 'You can't have all these guys here and not let them have a beer.' I remember afterwards, upstairs doing the dishes, and there was this line that formed of these guys. And this is what I love about hockey and what I loved about that team – they were all standing in line to say thank you. Neat. I was washing the dishes and they're going, 'Geez, thank you very much, it was great.' Here's Beezer and here's Jovie [Ed Jovanovski] and all these guys. It was like a family, and that filled him up so much when he had people at his house."

The fun might have lasted for Neilson if Clarke hadn't been lured back to the Flyers, getting leave from the final two years of his Florida contract. A head coach is always vulnerable when the man who hired him moves away. Bryan Murray replaced Clarke as GM, and it wasn't long – at the end of the second year – before Murray replaced Neilson with Doug MacLean, despite the fact

that Neilson had led his club to within a single point of a playoff berth in each of the first two seasons of the franchise.

Murray said the firing was not related to the team's performance but "a look toward the future of the franchise." In other words, Murray wanted a more open style of game in a market that had to work to attract fans now that the honeymoon was fading. Management also imagined a bigger role for young prospects like defenceman Jovanovski. Neilson had a full year left on his contract and was stunned over his dismissal.

"When you're underachieving, the coach often takes the hit," he said. "But when you're overachieving and you still get fired, it's tough."

After he was tossed, Neilson suggested he would have been amenable to changes. "I would have thought since we had a pretty good record, he'd give us the opportunity to listen to his new direction," he said. Nevertheless, Roger was stubborn enough to want to stick to his rather successful strategy of winning games with grinding veterans.

Murray offered Neilson a job as a scout with the Panthers. Roger declined and would soon be making tracks for St. Louis to become an assistant to his old pal Keenan.

Murray was vindicated for dumping Neilson, much as Neil Smith was in New York, when MacLean took the Panthers to the Stanley Cup finals in 1996, where they were swept by the Colorado Avalanche.

"It was hard for Roger to be let go, because we had just missed the playoffs," says Eakins. "The team was growing. Getting better. It was ready to take the next step. You can twist a hockey story any way you want, to the advantage of who's telling it, put any spin on it. Bryan made that decision and MacLean did get the team to the final, but Roger had as much to do with that success as anyone."

"The new guy wanted his own boy," says Craig Ramsay. According to Ramsay, the firing stung Roger because the staff

had been so involved in each element of building the franchise. "We weren't just coaching, we helped pick the players on that team."

Nichols calls the Florida firing "one of the biggest tragedies of Roger's life.

"It was really painful and hurtful for him. He never quite got over that. Every once in a while, out of the blue he'd say, 'Geez, what would have happened if I'd stayed in Florida?'"

Even at an occasion as sunny as his Hall of Fame induction in 2002, Roger couldn't help get in a last dig about his Florida dismissal. He thought he was in for a contract extension, he said, and instead he was in for the boot.

"I've been fired pretty much every way there is," Neilson said. "The ones that hurt the most are the ones where you don't figure it should happen, or out of the blue, like in Florida."

DOWNRIGHT SILLY IN PHILLY

The call from Bob Clarke in Philadelphia couldn't have come at a worse possible time. Or maybe it was the best possible time. Distraught as he was, Neilson himself wasn't sure.

It was early March, 1998. Roger had just buried the woman he believed was his last living relative, his beloved sister, Joan. Roger's mother had passed away several years earlier from Alzheimer's disease, and his father died years before that. And now Joanie. He found her a lovely resting place in Westminster Cemetery not far from their childhood home in north Toronto, knowing full well he'd one day be put to rest beside her.

In the hurly-burly that was Neilson's NHL life, it was easy to forget he had any relatives. He always talked of being "married to the game," that he didn't have time to commit to a wife and family. But in the off-season, and especially at Christmas time, Roger would arrange to meet with his closest friends, and with Joan, for the ritual celebration near Peterborough.

"It was important for Roger to have Joan there," says Ruby Bell, the mother of Brian Bell, who helped Roger deliver newspapers all those years ago. "That relationship was very precious. He said once, 'I don't think there was ever a day when we had words.'" Like Roger, Joan didn't marry, was deeply religious, and lived alone. Ruby called Joan a "smart, quiet" woman.

In the winter of 1994, Roger asked Ruby to look in on Joan, who hadn't been well. Ruby took Joan to Sunnybrook Hospital for tests.

"I used Roger's name," says Ruby, "because that always opened doors."

Joan was diagnosed with multiple myeloma, a form of cancer. She died in the first week of March 1998, just a few days before Clarke was on the phone offering Roger his first head-coaching job in three years. He had work, but no living relative to tell of it.

"My mother was born in South Africa, so maybe I have some people somewhere I don't know about," Neilson told the *Toronto Star*. "It was really tough to watch my sister. Really tough."

With six NHL cities in the rear-view mirror, Roger had learned a thing or two about survival. While there wasn't much he could have done about Harold Ballard or losing his support network in Florida, the lesson learned from Mark Messier was still fresh in his mind.

After alienating his captain in New York City, Roger wasn't going to make that mistake in Philadelphia with Eric Lindros. But then sometimes a guy can't win for losing. Two-thirds of the way through his second full season as Flyers head coach, Neilson's relationship with the Big E became an albatross around his neck, albeit an albatross the coach didn't want to shake, because Neilson was so fond of Lindros.

After his painful release from Florida, Neilson had the comfort of being reunited with his old Panthers GM, Clarke. Here was Roger's reward, finally, for lying low as an assistant coach to Mike

Keenan and then Joel Quenneville with the St. Louis Blues from 1995 to 1998.

Clarke hired Neilson in the spring of 1998 to replace Wayne Cashman. It took a year for the Flyers to look like a team that might do something, which, of course, is about when the wheels started to come off.

How different 1999-2000 could have been. This was a forty-five-win season, after all, the greatest number of victories Roger had known since his Rangers days. Lindros, a three-time recipient of the Bobby Clarke Trophy as team MVP (an irony presumably not lost on Clarke), seemed ready finally to live up to the hype that had followed him since his junior days in Oshawa. He'd scored forty goals the year before, using his size and power to bully his way into scoring positions. He was primed to lead this Flyers team, Messier-like, to Philadelphia's first Stanley Cup since 1975, when Clarke himself was the gap-toothed captain.

And the genial Neilson would be by his side all the way.

It was a fetching vision. Until it all unravelled.

From January through May of 2000, Lindros suffered no fewer than four head injuries and went to war against the volatile Clarke and the team's medical staff over his treatment. Suddenly, the letter C on the Big E's number-88 sweater stood for Concussions. Eventually, he had no C at all. Clarke removed it, fed up with Lindros and without Roger on the scene to smooth things over.

A different C-word had entered Roger's life just weeks before Eric's first concussion of the season. Neilson hardly imagined the worst when he slogged through training camp in the early fall of 1999 with a nagging cough and flu symptoms he couldn't seem to shake. Medical tests indicated an abnormally low red-blood-cell count, but it wasn't until a bone-marrow biopsy was done that the hard truth was learned. Cancer.

Neilson was diagnosed with multiple myeloma, a term with

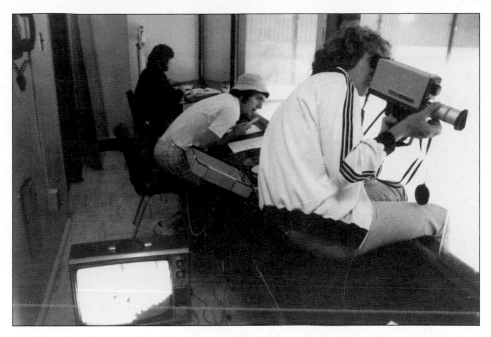

Roger calls the play-by-play while Al Dunford works the video camera at Roger's hockey school, where every participant was a star. *(Courtesy Roger Neilson estate)*

Eric Lindros, left, pictured here with Alex Anjelic, is always a big hit at Roger's hockey school in Lindsay. *(Courtesy Roger Neilson Hockey Camp)*

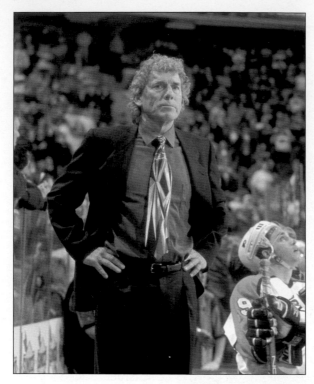

A classic Roger pose
behind the Philadelphia
Flyers bench. *(Hockey
Hall of Fame)*

Occasionally, Roger
disagreed with a game
official. Fellow future
Hall-of-Famer Mike
Gartner (wearing the "A")
stays cool while Neilson
melts down behind the
New York Rangers bench.
(Hockey Hall of Fame)

Roger could fall asleep anywhere, anytime. *(Courtesy Marshall Starkman)*

Nancy Nichols, with Roger behind, on a bus tour in Israel. They met in Dallas, 1977, and shared a ride of a lifetime. *(Courtesy Marshall Starkman)*

Shirtless in Masada. Roger knew the sites of the Middle East well enough to conduct his own tours. *(Courtesy Marshall Starkman)*

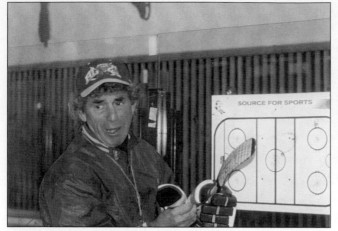

Giving a chalk talk at his hockey school in Metulla, Israel. Kids flocked in from the desert to skate with Neilson. *(Courtesy Marshall Starkman)*

A favourite pastime: soaking up sun. *(Courtesy Marshall Starkman)*

Getting muddy at the Dead Sea, along with Sal Guarna, left, and Kent Pearce. *(Courtesy Marshall Starkman)*

Captain Video was befuddled by modern conveniences such as cell phones. *(Courtesy Roger Neilson's Hockey School)*

Recipe for a Roger Neilson necktie: a slice of pizza with the works. *(Courtesy Roger Neilson estate)*

In his later years, Roger lived in this tricoloured track suit. *(Brent Foster, Ottawa Citizen)*

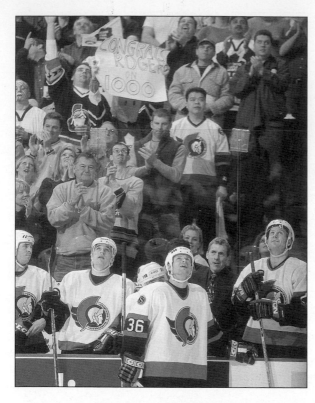

The Corel Centre crowd greets Roger at his 1,000th game as an NHL head coach in 2002. The Ottawa Senators' Jacques Martin stepped aside for the final two games of the regular season. *(Courtesy Ottawa Senators)*

Needing all his strength to receive the Order of Canada from Governor General Adrienne Clarkson. *(Pat McGrath, Ottawa Citizen)*

With broadcaster Bill Watters and the Great One, Wayne Gretzky. *(Courtesy Ottawa Senators)*

With Mike Keenan, who picked up in New York where Roger left off. *(Courtesy Ottawa Senators)*

With Scotty Bowman, who hired Roger to his first job in professional hockey. *(Courtesy Ottawa Senators)*

With two of his favourite Maple Leafs: Lanny McDonald and Darryl Sittler. *(Courtesy Ottawa Senators)*

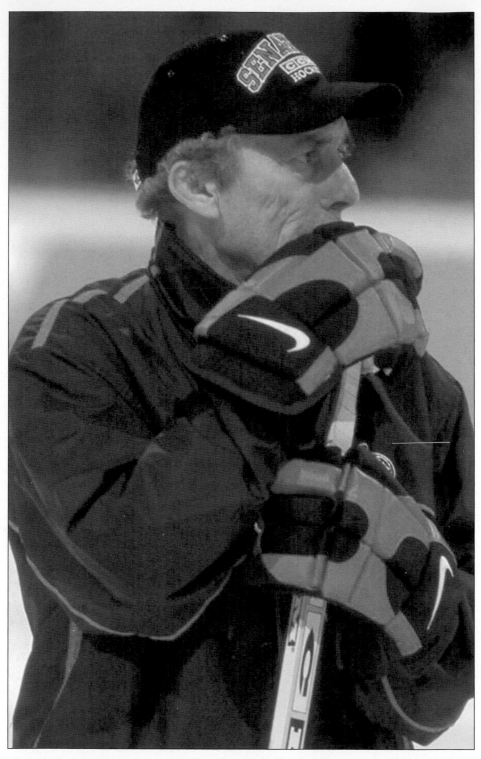

A pensive pose at practice. *(Courtesy Ottawa Senators)*

which he was unfortunately familiar, though it was a different strain of the form of cancer that had claimed the life of his sister, Joan. He was sixty-five.

On Thursday, December 9, 1999, after the Flyers defeated the Maple Leafs in Philadelphia, two Flyers team doctors were waiting for him outside his office. For Roger, seeing them was an ominous sign. He was scheduled to hear news about his bone-marrow biopsy the following morning. The look on the doctors' faces was revealing, even before they told him about the cancer.

Neilson spent the next little while on the telephone, calling many of the people closest to him. He found himself comforting them, rather than the other way around.

"It was a tough night," he admitted, his mind racing as quickly as the search engines on his computer for the terms "cancer" and "bone marrow" and "transplant."

Clarke, once a nasty leader on a team nicknamed the Broad Street Bullies, welled up with tears when he spoke about it to reporters.

Roger said his spirits soared the next morning when he discovered he wouldn't need to find a bone-marrow donor, that his own diseased marrow would be removed, cleansed, and replaced.

As only he could, Neilson informed his players the next day before practice at the Flyers training facility. He showed the team a video clip of defenceman Chris Therien, not in one of his finer moments. He was fighting a Leafs player the night before, but was off-balance, falling, and flailing. At one point, Therien had his back turned awkwardly to his opponent – then the tape leaped to the famous scene from *Monty Python's Holy Grail*, when the Black Knight is fighting on after losing his limbs, claiming it's "just a flesh wound."

Waiting until the laughter died down, Neilson silenced the room with three words.

"I have cancer."

That afternoon, the Flyers flew to Toronto for a return match with the Maple Leafs, this time on *Hockey Night in Canada*. At a news conference in his downtown Toronto hotel, Neilson put on a performance, one that would become familiar over the next few years. Keep it light. Keep it cheerful. Crack a joke, a little gallows humour, to ease the discomfort of those around him. Roger was surrounded by Flyers: the GM Clarke and players Lindros, John LeClair, Mark Recchi, and Eric Desjardins.

"I don't want people feeling sorry for me. That's crazy," said Neilson, his team sitting atop the Eastern Conference at the time with a 17-8-4-1 record. "It happens, and I'm trying not to worry about it. I've got strong religious beliefs. I believe God has plans for my life, and this happens to be part of it. If the plan is to beat it, then I'm going to give everything I've got to beat it. If that's not in the plans, then at least in the games up in Heaven, we won't have to put up with Kris King and Tie Domi."

Neilson called it a relief that he could continue to coach in the near future. And he didn't miss a beat when someone asked if anyone had suggested that he leave his bench duties.

"Several fans," he said.

An incurable cancer that causes about ten thousand deaths every year, multiple myeloma is treated by bone-marrow transplant and chemotherapy. Patients can live up to ten years. Although he wasn't naive enough to cling to false hope, Neilson also knew that there were rare cases that beat all odds. He felt as though he'd already known one.

"They found cancer in his dad when Roger was a teenager," says Harry Neale. "In those days, there wasn't a lot you could do. But it stopped itself, and Norman Neilson died of a heart attack quite a few years later [in his eighties]. I know Roger used to tell people who had cancer there are miracles that occur, you've gotta hope you're one of them, and his dad was, I guess."

Neilson stayed behind the Flyers bench until February 19, when he left the team to undergo stem-cell-transplant surgery. Craig Ramsay – Roger's assistant who had played for Roger in the NHL and in junior, and coached with him in Florida and Philadelphia – took over as interim head coach, with the understanding that Roger would return when he was well enough. That stipulation turned out to be a subjective, messy bit of business as Roger slipped into the next in a long line of soap opera scenarios.

This one would make the Messier situation in New York look like a walk in Central Park. In daylight.

Roger was told by his oncologist, Dr. Isadore Brodsky, that he could be back for the playoffs. Seemed like a simple enough short-term prognosis. Except that in the spring of 2000 nothing in Flyer-land was what it seemed to be. As the situation evolved, Neilson was sorely missed as the glue holding everything together. He was good with Clarke and close to Eric, but Eric was out of the picture, recuperating from a concussion that medical staff did not immediately identify as such.

From his sickbed, Neilson was trying his best to mend fences. He was playing Neil Smith's role now, trying to bring Lindros and Clarke together, who were just as hopelessly split as he and Messier had been. "A lot of things were said that should have been said in private," Neilson said later. "It wasn't a good situation."

Roger kept repeating that the team would welcome Lindros back when he was able to return. But when would Roger return? Initially, he was told it was reasonable to assume he could be back by the second round of the playoffs, if his team got that far. Then he was led to believe it might be sooner.

On March 21, three weeks before the Flyers met the Buffalo Sabres in the first round, Dr. Brodsky told reporters that Neilson was making remarkable progress. "The coach feels great today," said the chief of oncology at Hahnemann University Hospital in

Philadelphia. "We have stopped all intravenous. He's off all medications. His white-cell count is 10,000, which is more than it should be, so we are stopping all the drugs that he needs to stimulate his marrow. His marrow is perfectly engrafted.

"I want to see how he does next week," said Brodsky. "Depending on how he feels, he may rejoin the team a lot sooner than we thought."

On the eve of the playoffs, with Neilson proclaiming himself good to go, Clarke and the doctors were holding him off.

"I feel really good," said Neilson. "As a matter of fact, I feel good enough to coach, really, but the doctors and Bobby Clarke feel that I should wait till the second round, so during the first round I'll just help out in any way I can."

It was clear what was happening. The Flyers were doing quite well under Ramsay, thank you. Over the final twenty-five games of the season, the team went 16-8-1. Ramsay changed the lineup slightly and had his players taking shorter shifts. While the media circus raged with the twin stories of Lindros and Neilson, the team kept winning, whether in spite of or because of the temporary insanity. Veteran winger John LeClair said, "What else can happen? It became comical, really. It became easier and easier to block things out."

Clarke had no interest in making a change when the team was winning and playing with confidence. Roger Neilson, recuperating cancer patient, became the odd man out, watching games from the press box like a manager or a lowly scribe. He was disheartened and finding it more and more difficult to contain his frustration.

Famously, perhaps regrettably, Neilson would tell The Fan 590 radio station in Toronto after the Flyers defeated the Sabres in five games, "I don't think they want a cancer patient, who's a friend of Eric Lindros, behind the bench right now."

Incredibly enough, Clarke had a topper for that quote, speaking months later to another Canadian broadcast outlet, TSN in Toronto.

Clarke told Gord Miller that Neilson's contracting cancer "wasn't our fault. We didn't tell him to go get cancer. It's too bad that he did, and we feel sorry for him, but then he went goofy on us."

Clarke later explained to media in Philadelphia that what he meant by "goofy" was that Neilson had been engaging in behaviour that was very unlike Roger, angrily demanding his bench job back when the team felt he wasn't physically ready, then making the flippant remark on radio. Kent Pearce, one of Roger's Boys, was in Roger's office at the Flyers practice facility in Voorhees, New Jersey, when the conversation went down between Clarke and Neilson.

"Roger called up to Bobby Clarke's office and said, 'Well, I'm back and ready to go.' And Clarkey said, 'What do you mean?' And he said to Roger, 'Well, I don't think that's a good idea.'

"Roger hung up the phone and went right up. I was in Roger's office, Bobby Clarke's is right above, and through that thick floor I could hear them yelling. Unbelievable. Roger doesn't yell. Oh, man, he was heartbroken.

"When he was going through the bone-marrow transplant, the thing that kept him going was his team and him getting back to it. The doctors were saying, 'This is amazing, how quickly you're recovering.'"

Clarke came out of it looking like a bully cuffing a cancer patient. Few knew that the same bully quietly let Roger convalesce in Clarke's Florida condo after the surgery. Neilson flew to Florida in Clarke's private jet.

A little communication and a lot of common sense could have gone a long way to avoiding what became a horribly tangled mess between two hockey people who had worked closely together for two different NHL teams.

Lindros, not surprisingly, calls the Flyers' treatment of Neilson "awful."

Nancy Nichols was with Neilson during his treatments. "People have different reactions to sick people," says Nichols. "And it scared

Bobby Clarke. For a while there I could understand, because when Roger got out of the hospital after that stem-cell transplant and walked into the office . . . if you hadn't seen him for six weeks, you'd be shocked, too. In a lot of ways, a lot of these hockey general managers and presidents of the old-club hockey school, they haven't been to school, they haven't been educated, they're not sophisticated people. Bobby Clarke said to me one time, 'Geez, I can't believe I'm running this team. All I want to do is the hockey stuff, I don't want to do all the math.'

"So he had all the responsibility of making that team go, and I think he took one look at Roger and it scared the crap out of him. There was a lot of back-stabbing going on, saying the doctors said this, and the doctors were telling me something different. I was the one who was there every day. Brodsky would come in and talk about 'second round of the playoffs.' I was talking to Brodsky one day, and he said, 'You know, he's doing really great. I think we can probably get him back for the first round.'

"I said, 'Whatever you do, don't tell him that, because he will reset his goal.' Once they told him second round, he locked in on that. That's what he does. He's goal-oriented, and it's what he wanted other people to be. And damn if Brodsky didn't go out the next day and say to Roger, 'We're gonna have you back by the first round.' And Roger took hold of that. . . .

"In hindsight, they could have done it so much classier. Even if they put him behind the bench with Craig Ramsay to finish out the season and then said, 'Hey, guess what, we're sticking with Rammer.' But you know, Roger worked so hard to come back from that, and no one took into account his feelings about how important it was for him to go back and say, 'Look, I've got a new lease on life, and I'm just getting on with it.'

"Because Roger wanted that message out. For cancer patients. For cancer survivors. For people lacking in faith. Here's a guy who goes and has a stem-cell transplant and comes back and returns to

hockey. He had thousands of people, cancer people, that were calling him. I did an on-line report every day from the hospital. He really felt, not just for himself, that it was so important to come back from those things, and what kills me is that when Roger was rehabbing at Clarkey's place in Florida, there was no conversation between Clarke and Roger. No 'How are you doing?' I kept saying, 'Why don't you call in and just say, here's what I'm feeling, and I'm going to be ready for the first round.' . . . I always call it the men-will-be-boys syndrome. It's just too emotional. And the team got hot. . . . You know, I can sort of understand both sides. But in the middle, I'm like, 'Why can't you guys just get in one room, shut the door, and have it out? Nobody even needs to know what's said. Just say it to each other.' It just turned into a mess. And I don't think Clarkey will ever live it down."

Clarke gets a lot of abuse for his handling of Roger's cancer situation, much of it deserved, but letting Ramsay continue to run the team when Neilson wanted to return wasn't entirely unlike Roger filling in for Harry Neale in Vancouver eighteen years earlier. After his suspension, Neale could have resumed his job as Canucks head coach, but he stayed with the hot hand, his assistant, Neilson, scheduled to become the head coach the next season anyway.

Clarke stayed with Ramsay, whose team went 16-8-1 down the stretch and reached the Eastern Conference finals in the playoffs. The Flyers got knocked out – literally in the case of Eric Lindros – by Scott Stevens and the New Jersey Devils.

Sadly, Neilson had been close to signing a new contract in Philadelphia as recently as January 2000, according to his agent, Rob Campbell. "Clarke had spoken to us about an extension, and we'd basically agreed to it, with [Flyers owner Ed] Snider, when Roger got sick with cancer," says Campbell. "They reneged because he was ill." The Flyers denied that contention.

Campbell was at a meeting in San Diego when Mike Keenan called to tell him about Roger's diagnosis. Campbell jumped on a

plane to meet Roger in Toronto. They talked for five hours at the Westin Harbour Castle Hotel.

Poor Clarke. He couldn't escape Campbell, who has a string of coaching clients thanks to Neilson. Campbell negotiated the contract of current Flyers coach Ken Hitchcock, and says, "Clarke wanted nothing to do with me. And yet, Clarke doesn't speak ill of Roger."

For all that got silly in Philly in the spring of 2000, the doctors and Clarke and Roger's friends and associates probably agree on one thing. Resuming his head-coaching duties in the playoffs would not have been the best thing for Roger's health.

As it turned out, Neilson may have escaped just in time.

The Flyers struggled at the start of the 2000-01 season, and Ramsay was fired after twenty-eight games and replaced by Bill Barber, another short-term answer.

By now, Neilson was safely in Ottawa with a coach's dream. A contract longer than life itself.

Roger's Boys

O*xford* and *Webster's* don't have entries for the term "Roger's Boys." Not yet, anyway.

But the vast web of Roger Neilson's friends and associates understands what it means. They all know if they are or were one.

To be one of Roger's Boys meant entering his unusual world of recreation and adventure, usually at a young age. Often, it was a life sentence.

You were a student in one of his classes, played hockey or baseball for him. Or you attended his hockey school.

You helped him deliver papers in north Toronto on what grew to be one of the world's largest, and certainly most famous, *Globe and Mail* routes.

Maybe you were competing in a track-and-field event when Roger saw the potential to convert you to a baseball player.

You might have been the son of one of his assistant coaches.

Typically, he saw something, a spark, some athletic ability; he recognized the potential for a contribution to the cause. He saw trouble at home and a boy needing an outlet.

Schools, hockey rinks, ballparks, playgrounds – these were the seedbeds for the hundreds of youth who came to be known as Roger's Boys. Many of them today are grown men, fathers of children who also came to join Roger's band. Had he not died prematurely at age sixty-nine, Roger would soon have been tapping a third generation of young followers. Ron Smith, Roger's first NHL assistant coach, has grandchildren. Those youngsters – one of them named Tate Neilson Smith ("Good thing it's a boy with a name like Neilson," said Roger, dryly, when told of the honour) – are just a few years away from potential rink-rat duty.

It's been established that Roger was a lifelong coach, beginning when he was just seventeen and attending university classes in Hamilton. But like any college coach, he doubled as a recruiter – not for college teams, but for competitive amateur organizations in minor hockey or baseball.

Once Roger tapped someone as a youth recruit, there was no end to the games and tasks and adventures that followed. Organized hockey. Rog road hockey. Youth baseball. Recreational ping-pong tournaments. A cottage in need of painting. Papers to deliver. Rink rats were needed for his hockey schools and the million tasks therein. It took extra hands to organize his annual coaches' clinic.

Join the club. See the world. Be a part of group adventure trips up the river, or across the border, if not around the world.

In this age of general mistrust, amateur coaches are routinely screened by police before they're allowed to coach children. The gross misdeeds of Graham James in the Western Hockey League twenty years ago, revealed only years later, put parents and youth sporting initiatives on high alert for any kind of suspicious

behaviour between coach and athlete. Minor-hockey coaches today are taught in Speak Out courses not to touch players or be in situations where they might be alone with a youngster in a dressing room or a car.

If he were subjected to a modern Speak Out awareness session of Hockey Canada, Roger Neilson likely would have scratched his curly head in wonder. For most of his coaching and instructional career, Roger openly roughhoused and wrestled with his kids, he took them on trips, treated them as though they were an endless collection of nephews, cousins, pals. Not once was his character called into question.

Upfront and charming, Roger had a way of instilling trust, almost instantaneously.

Writer Jay Teitel described Roger's "candid and humble authority," which won over children and parents alike.

Ruby Bell's son, Brian, was a student of Roger's at Bayview Junior High in north Toronto. He was also one of Roger's *Globe* carriers, played midget hockey for him on the Toronto North Lions, and was part of a motoring adventure to California and the Grand Canyon in the early 1960s.

"I was so intrigued by Roger wanting to take the boys on trips," said Ruby, who quickly adopted the dynamic young coach from Sheppard Avenue as a member of the family. "I thought, 'How magnificent.' They would never have seen these things otherwise. Roger was responsible, but he was also tuned into that era."

He was also tuned into their music, which in the 1960s and 1970s was lots of Neil Young.

And did Brian Bell think of Roger as a teacher, coach, or newspaper boss?

"He was more like a best friend," he says, echoing a common refrain among Roger's Boys.

Dick Todd, who would eventually follow Roger's lead to become coach of the Peterborough Petes, was another early Roger's

Boy. Todd was on the newspaper route and a catcher and pitcher on Roger's baseball teams.

"At the age of 10 my life was about to be altered in ways I couldn't even imagine," Todd wrote in a tribute to Neilson that appeared in the *Peterborough Examiner*. "My 12-year-old neighbour announced he was going to the park for baseball tryouts and I could tag along if I wished. The tryouts were for a peewee team that would consist of 11- and 12-year-olds. Somehow the coach saw something in this scrawny 10-year-old and invited me to join the team. Of course the coach was Roger Neilson, and in 1955, I officially became one of 'Roger's Boys.'

"My mother was very ill and spent much of the next four years in the hospital. My father devoted what time he had to caring for my mother. Being somewhat at loose ends, I gravitated to baseball and to Roger. He intuitively knew what to say and how to make a lonely 10-year-old feel good about himself. He quickly became my coach, mentor, surrogate parent, and very special friend. I often attended church with Roger and he helped me develop a set of values I have carried with me throughout my life.

"In 1964, with Roger as coach, I pitched the final game when we won the National Junior Baseball Championship for Eastern Canada. That winter, thanks to Roger's years of training, coaching and encouragement I achieved a childhood dream of signing a contract with a professional sports team. I signed with the Pittsburgh Pirates and in doing so I believe I was the first of Roger's Boys to sign a pro contract in any sport. Shortly after signing with the Pirates, my professional aspirations were dashed when I tore my rotator cuff. I was devastated as I had dreamt of this opportunity for years and I had worked so hard. Once again Roger consoled me and helped me discover other avenues in life."

Those avenues would include a coaching career, following in Neilson's footsteps, that would bring Todd a Memorial Cup ring,

a Calder Cup ring, and, in 1994, a Stanley Cup ring, as an assistant to Mike Keenan with the New York Rangers.

Todd dedicated all of his championships to Neilson, not that he didn't occasionally feel the jab of the coach's dry wit. Todd remembers having his catching career assessed this way, in hindsight, by Roger: "He said that when I was 10, I was the best 10-year-old catcher in the city of Toronto. At 11, I was middle of the road and by 12, I was the worst."

Doug Peacock played minor hockey for Roger in Toronto, followed Neilson's career path into education, and, coincidentally or not, wound up being principal of the high school in Peterborough where Neilson taught for several years.

Rob Campbell was one of many young softball players Roger would convert to hardball. Roger taught Campbell how to hit; in turn, Campbell grew to pitch contracts for Roger as his lawyer, agent, and dear friend.

Campbell was ten when Roger invited him for his first baseball tryout, a frightening experience Campbell remembers to this day. It was like a scene out of the *Our Gang* TV series with Spanky and the Little Rascals.

"It was arranged I'd get picked up at a certain intersection at 6:00 p.m. the next night," says Campbell, sitting in his tony office in downtown Toronto. "So I'm standing there, carrying my glove, and this blue Volkswagen van squeals to a stop, a door slides open, and Roger says, 'Get in.' Sitting right across from me is this German shepherd that looks like a wolf to me. The dog yawns and he's got teeth on him like a dinosaur."

The dog, of course, was Roger's beloved Jacques.

Campbell didn't move an inch until he was safely out the door.

For the next ten years, Campbell played baseball for Rog, attended law school with Neilson's encouragement, and represented his business interests, including NHL contracts, until Roger's death.

Al Dunford was a former Roger rink rat who joined Neilson on the Toronto Maple Leafs staff as travel secretary in the late 1970s. Dunford would ultimately coach a school hockey team at St. Andrew's College in Aurora, Ontario, and directed numerous candidates to Roger's hockey school, including the current hockey camp manager and goaltending coach Marshall Starkman.

"There's that six-degrees-of-separation theory at work with Roger," says Dunford. "Some people hadn't even met Roger, but knew people that knew him."

Over time, Roger the recruiter had a lot of recruiting help. Roger's influence grew like a web, in which the keen and unsuspecting became entangled.

Kris King is a good example. In the early 1980s, King was a rookie on a Peterborough Petes team coached by Todd. "I came out of Gravenhurst Junior C and needed ice time," says King, sitting at a picnic table outside the Lindsay arena during a 2003 hockey school appearance. "We didn't have any summer ice in Muskoka. Roger and Todd had been scheming, I figured out later, looking for camp counsellors. Dick said it would be excellent for me, that I was going to get all this ice time.

"I ended up working five weeks of pure hell. I got my ice time, but I also had a job that was long hours and didn't pay very much.

"From then on, I was one of Roger's guys. I was sixteen and I've been with him ever since."

Disciple loyalty was consistently rewarded.

Neilson recruited King again, to play for him on the New York Rangers team he coached from 1989 to 1993. It was just two days after Neilson himself had become a Ranger.

"I was just a second-year pro, and I'm sure the trade had a lot to do with our relationship through hockey school. He taught me how to be a pro. I was a part-time player in Detroit. Played over-age with Peterborough. Marc Crawford. Dallas Eakins. Colie Campbell. Jody Hull. Me. We were his guys, and he looked out for us."

Brian Kilrea, Hall of Fame coach of the OHL Ottawa 67's, always says he's as proud of the players who went on to productive jobs outside the game as he is of his NHL performers.

So it was with Neilson. He was thrilled to see some of his young recruits, some former rats, others Petes, reach the NHL, people like King, Todd, Doug Jarvis, Bob Gainey, Craig Ramsay, Rick MacLeish, Greg Millen, Joe Murphy, Steve Smith, John Druce, and others – but he was equally proud of the rats and players who became teachers, accountants, ministers.

Larry Pearson, Paul Bedford, Jim Faulkner, Dave Clements, and the rest of the Peterborough-area gang were central figures in a kind of Neilson task force in the late 1960s and early 1970s. Now, they're the parents of camp rats and instructors. Pearson and Bedford remember accompanying Roger on a drive to Buckhorn Lake to check out a log cabin property for sale.

"Paul and I are country kids, in grade nine and ten, and he's asking our opinion of the place," says Pearson. "Thank goodness Paul's dad, Harry, knew what he was doing and took a look at it. I remember going down the steps to the water, one of the steps was out of line. Roger went down with his dad. He figured if his dad could get down without stumbling, it was okay."

At his home on Chemong Lake, Roger was constantly building additions and adding recreational facilities so that visitors could enjoy them. Eventually, he built it into a seven-bedroom, three-bathroom, 6,000-square-foot waterfront resort for Neilson friends in the know. Parents brought their children. Schools and organizations sent their teams, which stayed overnight during tournaments. Guests ranged from visiting missionaries to the local OHL Petes. Roger's was a recreational halfway house that frowned upon alcohol, tobacco, and words of four letters.

Kids played pool, table tennis, outdoor tennis, ball hockey on a rink near the boathouse, water polo. They swam in the L-shaped pool, soaked in the hot tub, and splashed along a

260-foot shoreline. Tubing behind Roger's boat was always popular and usually ended with a raid on a freezer filled with a year's supply of ice cream. If Neilson wasn't driving the boat, he was sitting at his desk, ball cap pulled over his head, watching videos, doing paperwork, talking on the phone, while mayhem ensued all around him.

Sometimes, the joint was packed and Roger wasn't even home.

The house could sleep more than twenty, excluding floor space. Neilson's office was attached to the remodelled, open-concept kitchen and dining room overlooking the swimming pool and lake. Nancy Nichols told a visiting reporter that Neilson built a $200,000 extension to the house in 1999 so he'd have room for a shuffleboard table.

The next summer, an *Ottawa Citizen* reporter visited Roger's house after Neilson had been hired by the Senators. "Sometimes, I'll open up a door and see someone sleeping that I didn't even know was here," Neilson told the reporter at the outset of hockey camp season. "I don't mind. There's lots of room."

As the Peterborough Petes head coach from 1967 to 1977, Roger found a steady supply of helpers at Crestwood Secondary, where he taught. Pearson, Bedford, and the rest were the usual suspects.

"Now we were going from playing on his baseball team to, 'Can you travel with the Petes and do some stats?'" says Clements. "It was like, 'Hey, this is getting better and better.'"

If the Petes were travelling on a school night, Roger would order up bacon-and-tomato sandwiches for his young helpers. If they got home late, they'd sleep at his house and he'd drive them into school in the morning. They'd then shower at school.

"Julie Burch was our home ec teacher," says Pearson. "Sometimes when she'd find out we were out late on a Petes trip, she'd make up a meal for all his little rats."

In his last couple of years of high school, Pearson says he spent as much time at Roger's home as he did at his own. When Larry's father died, Roger made a rare appearance inside the Pearson home. Larry's mother blurted out, "Well, if it isn't Roger Neilson, the guy that raised my son."

Dave Ap Clements remembers his mother being mildly jealous of the time Dave spent away from him with Roger. But their country homes came to feel like dull places compared to Roger's world. Whatever the wee hour, the wheels were always turning.

"One night he called on the way back from a game in Niagara Falls," says Clements. "I didn't do the road trip, but he called to say he would be back by 1:00 a.m. and wanted the group to meet at the Memorial Centre for a little game. I remember calling the guys: Al Dunford was out on a farm by Stewart Hall [south of Peterborough], and other guys were trying to arrange a car pool. The Petes bus got back at 1:00 or 1:30 and we played shinny till 3:00 or 4:00 in morning."

Roger's recruits are the first to admit that their fearless leader wasn't necessarily drawn to the best and brightest, whether as hockey school employees or professional players. Perhaps to his own detriment, Neilson had a renowned penchant for grinders, workers, ordinary people who threw themselves at a task much as he did. "He was a very loyal guy," says Clements. "Once he brought somebody on board, he might not be best, but he was going to keep that person, work with him."

Clements laughs. "We're all part of that formula. He'll keep bringing them back, try to make them a better person, a better employee. He looked for character people. In a lot of circumstances, he felt character was more important than raw talent. He wanted good people. But he also had people under his wing that weren't great people and tried to make them good."

Rob Campbell goes one further: "He had a soft spot for rogues and rascals."

Neilson had no shortage of prodigal sons. Some of them worked out. Some remained a work in progress. His friends say Roger had a blind spot for some of the young characters he endorsed.

Ruby Bell was astounded at some of the goings-on. "He was very lenient with those kids. He would let them just run around. The kitchen plates were a half-inch thick so they wouldn't break. To me, he was far too lenient. They got away with murder.

"You'd say, 'Roger, the kids are just wrecking the place,' and he'd say, 'Ah, they're okay.'"

Neilson thought nothing of taking a group of his hockey school staff to Hawaii for an all-expenses-paid-by-Roger vacation. And if some of those guests ran up a group telephone bill in excess of $1,500, Roger shrugged it off. Other disciples ventured to Europe and Africa with Neilson as tour guide. As Dunford says, "If you were lucky enough to be a part of Roger's inner circle, you got to travel with him. And I was a part of that."

Though he was forgiving of most boys-will-be-boys behaviour, Neilson had his personal list of mortal offences. Devin Smith says that Roger didn't have to spell out the rules. "You knew what not to do. A couple of guys messed up at his camp with drinking or girls and they got fired."

And yet Roger always made time for sinners, especially when their sins were committed on someone else's watch. Smith remembers Roger would come into Vancouver and take the Smiths, the Ervins, and Todd Ervin's friends out to dinner. One of the group was a wayward soul who wound up in jail. But he wrote Roger from prison, and Roger, the world's most reliable correspondent, wrote him back.

The best and worst of Neilson's recruits say they wanted to be better people after meeting Roger, after seeing how he lived, after benefiting from his influence.

Chad Schella, one of Neilson's many success stories, works for the Ottawa Senators Foundation, leading the drive to build Roger's House, a palliative youth-care facility to be located near the children's hospital in Ottawa. "You didn't want to let Rog down," says Schella, a former camp rat who looked to his uncle and to Neilson as his primary male mentors after his parents divorced. "I can't put into words what he meant to me, and I'm just one of many people to say that. I miss him every day."

Pearson reflects on Roger's life and assigns him the label of Youth Missionary. "He looked to see how he could possibly influence someone in a positive way. He used sports as his medium, but also travel, history, general-interest things, and life habits."

Though his faith ran through him like a major artery, Neilson didn't force religion on his young running mates. He might suggest they pick up a book, namely the Good Book, but it wasn't until his later years that he would consistently impress upon them, in person, in letters, the importance of faith.

Rob Campbell was excited about his children getting a chance to visit Roger at his cottage, so that "through osmosis, they would see how he led his life.

"I was always impressed how it didn't matter if he was talking to the prime minister or a ten-year-old kid at camp. It was the same approach. There were no airs put on. You try to calculate, through hockey schools, the NHL, and teaching, how many thousands of people he interacted with in a positive way."

While he was a legendary cheapskate on the small stuff, Roger could be exceedingly generous, including to his rink rats. When Landry Smith, coach Ron Smith's son, graduated from high school, Roger gave him a watch he'd received at a World Hockey Championship. It was worth about $4,000. Roger told Landry that if he wanted to keep the watch, that was fine, but he offered him the option of selling it and using the money toward his post-secondary education.

From the stories that go around, Roger was more generous than the provincial government with loans and grants for education. Dozens of young students have stories of Roger funding programs, lending cash, and writing letters of recommendation.

None of Roger's Boys will forget the way their life changed after meeting Roger Neilson. This was especially true for some of those in the inner circle.

DARREN KEILY

Darren Keily doesn't put a Krispy Kreme coating on it. "Without Roger's influence on my life, who knows what would have happened to me?" he says. "Quite honestly, I'd probably be in jail or dead at this point."

Darren Keily is a big man, barrel-chested. At thirty-five, he's thoughtful, serious, and scarred from the deaths of loved ones.

Slowly, tapping the same grassroots as the master, Keily has forged a career in hockey, albeit one that has generally been supported by a part-time job. In a development that made his heart swell with pride, Keily was named assistant coach of the OHL Peterborough Petes just weeks after Neilson died. Roger's Petes.

Before the 2003-04 OHL season was over, Keily became the interim head coach and was assured a future role with the organization. When the new head coach was introduced, it was yet another of Roger's Boys, Dick Todd.

Todd first met Roger as a ten-year-old, played baseball and delivered newspapers for him in Toronto, and joined him as a trainer with the Petes before becoming the most successful junior coach in Peterborough history during the 1980s. Now Todd was back, ending a brief retirement after seven years in the NHL, working with two others who learned the game under Neilson: Keily and Petes general manager Jeff Twohey.

The wheels keep turning in Roger's world. It's as though he's orchestrating this master plan from above. Putting pieces in place. Getting his guys where they belong.

The pattern isn't lost on Keily.

Typical of one of Roger's Boys, Keily was about ten when he first came under Roger's influence. The Keilys had just moved to Port Hope from Meaford, Ontario. Darren's father, Bill, was a maintenance supervisor at Trinity College, and in the late 1970s the college became the annual summer home of Roger's hockey school.

During the course of the five-week camps, Roger got to know Bill Keily and Keily's son, who was keen to jump into goal on those occasions when there was a shortage of goalies for scrimmages.

Although he wasn't aware of it at the time, Darren was a frequent topic of discussion between Roger and Bill Keily as their friendship grew. Bill suffered from chronic heart disease and didn't expect to live a long life. He and Roger had an understanding that if anything happened to Bill, Roger would look out for Darren, provide him with guidance and support as he saw fit.

Bill's heart might have been weak, but his instincts were impeccable in considering Roger Neilson a potential mentor for Darren.

Darren had just become a teenager when his father suffered a fatal heart attack. On cue, Roger swept onto the scene. It was nearly time for the annual hockey camp, and Roger took the thirteen-year-old Darren with him to the airport in Toronto to meet another rink rat Neilson had befriended in Vancouver. The year was 1982 and Roger was flying high. He'd just led the Canucks, bigger underdogs than Roger's own mutts, to the Stanley Cup final against the New York Islanders.

"You're going to get along great," Roger told Darren about the incoming lad.

He was right, of course.

The kid's name was Todd Ervin.

Wistfully, Keily recalls Roger and Todd and the summer they helped a boy in distress escape his worries.

"Todd and I were inseparable," he says. "Between Roger and Todd, they kept my mind so busy, the grieving process was pretty quick."

The trio took boat trips up the Trent-Severn Waterway. They went to ball games, had barbecues, and, of course, they worked together at Roger's hockey school.

Years later, when Roger's summer holidays included an annual trip to Hawaii, Keily was part of the extravaganza six or seven times. Hawaii was fun, outside the box as life with Roger always was, and yet Darren's favourite memories are centred on the two summers he spent with Todd and Roger. Cruising up the Trent-Severn. Overnighting in Orillia. Scared to death they might not make it across Lake Couchiching.

Between summers, when Roger was back coaching in the NHL, life was more difficult for Keily. In the late 1980s, he was approaching twenty and still listless. "Not that I was out robbing stores or anything," he says, "but I'd quit school. I wasn't big on school, I could have gone a lot further down that road. God knows what would have happened without his influence. I'm fortunate. Really fortunate."

The only school that captured Keily's attention was the five-week program that bore Neilson's name. It was at the hockey school that Keily felt a sense of community and belonging.

"It was a blast every summer," he says. "You'd almost cry on the last day. You'd think, 'I don't want to go back to school. I want to stay and do this the rest of my life.'"

On the last day of the high school calendar, Keily would instantly make tracks for Roger's house near Peterborough. On the day before school started up again in September, Roger would drop Darren back at his mother's home in Port Hope.

Keily spent eight summers working at Roger's camp and living at his house, with any number of other squatters.

"At Roger's house, you lived there for nothing, but he always had a million things for you to do. Planning for the hockey school. The coaches' clinic. Looking after the house.

"It was great for him and great for us. He had people around, which he loved. You feel pretty honoured to be living at Roger's house."

In 1989, the year Roger became head coach of the New York Rangers, Darren, now twenty, continued to struggle during the long season between camps. He was out of work, and so discouraged with his life that he quit playing hockey.

Not knowing where else to turn, Keily called Roger in New York. Neilson put him on a train to the big city.

Keily came under Neilson's care at that point – not that he was an overnight success. Rob Campbell, Neilson's lawyer and agent, remembers wandering through New York City with Roger and Colin Campbell at 3:00 in the morning during one particular visit, trying to track down Keily out on a night crawl.

During the hockey season, particularly when he was a head coach, Roger was insanely busy. He didn't have a lot of free time to devote to Darren, but he found him some work at Madison Square Garden, helping out the trainers, those behind-the-scene characters who make an NHL hockey team tick.

At the end of the 1989-90 season, Roger called Darren and told him that the trainers had enjoyed having him around – another way of saying he had pulled his weight. For the first time, Darren had himself a full-time job in hockey, as an assistant equipment manager with the New York Rangers.

For the next two-and-a-half years, through Neilson's tenure in New York, Darren lived at the coach's houses in Rye and then Mamoraneck and worked at MSG. He'd never before experienced this sense of calm and control during a winter hockey

season – that was usually reserved for summertime and Roger's camps.

"It's something about Roger. When you're with Roger, you're just a better person. Everybody swears a little bit, but when you're with Roger, you don't even think about swearing. Everything seems a little easier to deal with. Being in New York with him got me back on track.

"Those two years were absolutely key for me. I haven't been out of hockey since."

Darren remembers Rye being "like the Beverly Hills of New York." Neilson had a guest house overlooking Long Island Sound. The second year, they moved to nearby Mamoraneck.

In nearly three years of Big Apple living, Darren says, he and Roger never cooked a meal. Roger loved eating at New York's diners, and he wasn't home during what most people considered the dinner hour.

Living with Roger, Darren got a first-hand look at the man's work ethic and values. Home at midnight. Up at 6:30. Back to the rink. Church on Sunday. Bible study Mondays at dawn. Unlike the rest of the world, Neilson seemed to have time for everything and everybody.

"I'm such a worrywart," says Keily. "I need to be here, I need to be early. But when you were with Rog, you knew you were never going to be on time and you didn't worry about it. You just knew that it was going to work out, and if it didn't, then he would fix it. There's just a comfort zone being with Roger."

Keily was with Roger for one of the toughest times of his life, when he was fired by the Rangers. At the same time, Roger's beloved dog, Mike, was deathly ill. Keily was with Neilson when he took him to an animal hospital to see if anything could be done.

Darren looked up to see Rog coming out of the vet's office, tears running down his face, carrying Mike in a cardboard box.

In the span of a few days, Neilson was out of work and had lost his dog.

Colin Campbell and his wife, Heather, visited Roger to see how he was doing. They arrived in time to see Neilson and his long-time Peterborough pal, Mac Brick, loading Mike's body, sealed in an airtight bag, into the back of Roger's truck. Roger was determined to bury Mike at home, in his backyard, a tribute to Mike's status.

"This isn't going to work, Rog," Campbell told him. "They aren't going to let you cross the border with a dead dog in the back of your truck."

Of course, Roger did just that.

Keily completed the season in New York, then went to Cornwall, Ontario, to work with Jacques Martin as equipment manager of the Aces, the AHL farm team of the Colorado Avalanche. After two years, Rob Campbell and Roger helped Keily land a job in Barrie, Ontario, with Bert Templeton, the legendary major junior coach, and the OHL Colts. Templeton is best known across the country as the coach of Canada's world junior team that brawled with the Russians in 1987.

Although he had a reputation for being difficult – hard on his players and cold with reporters – Templeton was a solid family man and an ideal mentor for someone learning the game. In his third year with the Colts, Templeton advised Keily that he was wasting his time as a trainer – and promoted him to assistant coach.

In 1999, Keily followed Templeton to the Sudbury Wolves of the OHL. For Templeton, second only to Brian Kilrea in major junior victories, it would be his final hockey stop. Templeton was fired by the Wolves after the 2002-03 season in a nasty separation that forced an ailing, highly respected coach to fight for the balance owing on his contract.

Just before Neilson died in the summer of 2003, Templeton, sixty-three, discovered he was suffering from metastatic renal cell

carcinoma, a fancy way of saying he didn't have long to live.

Keily wasn't aware of Templeton's condition when he drove to Peterborough to be at Roger's bedside for most of his final days. Nearing the end, Keily called Templeton in Sudbury to give him the bad news, that it wouldn't be long now.

Templeton replied, "Darren, I also have some bad news . . ."

Now Keily was forced to deal with the looming loss of yet another important male figure in his world.

"It was tough knowing that Roger, who had been the biggest influence on my life, wasn't going to be around for long," Keily told the *Peterborough Examiner*. "Then to hear Bert, who was the second-most influential person in my life, was probably going to go down a similar road was, and still is, pretty overwhelming.

"From a selfish standpoint, I was thinking, 'Man, here goes another person that I lean on.' That was the most difficult for me and still is. Whether it be a life problem at home, or a hockey problem, or just someone to talk to, those two guys have been there for me. Roger since I was eleven years old and Bert for the last eight years. I think sometimes people think that I just worked for Bert. As time progressed, it was more of a friendship."

Rob Campbell used to hear from Templeton about Keily's progress. "He couldn't speak more highly about Darren," said Campbell, "and Bert had pretty tough standards."

Bert Templeton could be tough, period, crusty and quick to cuss. But even "Bramalea Bert," as he was known in Toronto for his gritty Junior B teams in the 1970s, fell under the Neilson spell. In his later years, Templeton became a Christian and fought, sometimes in vain, against the urge to use foul language when he got angry behind the bench.

Keily got to know a different Templeton, a kind, loyal man who wasn't afraid to hold the hand of his wife, Sandy, in public.

"If I can be half the man either of those guys was and half the coach they were, I'll be doing okay," says Keily.

Neilson and Templeton would be proud of Keily today, the newly appointed assistant general manager and assistant coach of the Petes. Keily is married, settled, and developing into a sound hockey man. And he hasn't yet run out of mentors. With Dick Todd – fifty-nine but still a Roger's Boy at heart – back coaching in Peterborough, Keily is in good company.

If they have any rough patches, they can always pull out one of a thousand Roger Neilson stories and be able to laugh.

"You're never going to meet another person like him," Keily says of Roger. "There's an awful lot of good people in the world, but I don't know anybody who's even close to him."

TODD ERVIN

Roger Neilson was a godfather, "uncle," mentor, counsellor, friend, coach, teacher, paper-route czar, and tour guide to thousands of young people in his lifetime.

Of all the rink rats, hall monitors, spark plugs, and other young men who came under Roger's guidance, there was one protegé who held a unique place in his heart.

His name was Todd Ervin. The boy underneath the permanent California Angels cap.

Todd was the son Roger might have had, but didn't.

Bright, dark-haired, blue-eyed, handsome, quick, engaging, Todd Ervin lit up the world like a shooting star on a summer night, enthralling his audience in a brief shower of glory.

"This kid was really funny," says Devin Smith, a friend and neighbour of the Ervin family in the Vancouver suburb of Port Moody. "Everybody loved him. The girls loved him. He was a good athlete. Of all the guys who were close to Rog, he was the closest."

Devin Smith's father, Ron, was a long-time assistant coach of Neilson's, including with the Canucks of the early 1980s. Devin's older brother, Landry, was Todd's best friend. Together they played epic games of road hockey on the side streets of Port

Moody. Neilson got to know Todd through the Smiths. Through road hockey.

By then, Landry was already a rink rat at Roger's hockey school, and the Smith brothers would sometimes stay at Roger's house in North Vancouver for a weekend.

If the brothers knew Roger was coming over for a Sunday dinner at their home, they made sure they had a road-hockey game going by the time the coach pulled in the driveway.

"Roger would play with us for hours, then he'd usually fall asleep at the dinner table," says Devin. "Or he'd go sit on the couch and fall asleep. Later, my mom would cut his hair."

Lynn Ervin, Todd's mother, remembers coming home one day to hear her husband, Nate, say, "You're not going to believe who's in the basement." It was, of course, Neilson.

Roger and the gang had just come in from a game of road hockey. It was the summer of 1981, and Neilson was about to start his first season with the Canucks as an assistant to Harry Neale.

Todd, then twelve, connected with Roger.

The boy called him Rajah, as though he were a descendant of an Indian prince. He would tease Neilson, poke fun at his foibles. Laugh at his minor injuries.

"He would say stuff to Rog, to get a rise out of him, that no one else would have got away with," says Devin.

The Ervins had moved to Port Moody in 1972. Lynn and Nate Ervin met at the University of Colorado, and Todd, their only son, was born in Tennessee.

From infancy, Todd had asthma. By the time he was five or six, the condition had improved, but he didn't lose his sensitivity to allergens and used a puffer.

It was easy for his parents to forget he had asthma. Todd was a superior athlete, busy, active. When he was about fifteen, Todd told his parents he was going try out for an elite local soccer team – as a goaltender, a position he hadn't played. It seemed a little far-fetched,

even for a quick study like Todd. But with the help of a goaltender friend he sharpened his skills and made the team. His coach would later tell the Ervins that, because of his versatility, Todd was the best athlete he'd coached.

Playing competitive soccer meant giving up hockey for a season; the Ervins weren't going to let two overlapping sports contend with Todd's school work.

Summertime meant Rajah time, as Todd routinely flew east to join Neilson's hockey camp, which was then in Port Hope, Ontario.

Todd celebrated five of his birthdays at Roger's camp, starting with his thirteenth.

"Before that first camp, Roger came to us to ask permission to fly him east," says Lynn. "Roger said, 'Todd is young, but I think he's mature enough to handle it, though I wouldn't think of doing it without your okay.'

"He was not yet thirteen, and it was a big trip for him, but we said we have to let him do it and see how it goes. And it was wonderful."

When Todd arrived home from camp, Roger called the house and talked to Lynn when the boy wasn't around. Neilson wondered if there were any issues with Todd, such as getting homework completed, that he might be able to reinforce. Without hinting about any parental conversation, Roger wrote Todd a letter, reminding him to "always listen to your parents . . . and make sure you get your homework done."

"And, of course, he would listen to Roger," says Lynn.

Lynn remembers once asking Todd if Roger seemed "like a best friend."

"No," he replied, "Landry is my best friend."

"Well, then, is he like a second father?"

"No, I have a dad. I don't know how to classify it, but maybe like a brother or a soulmate."

"They were," says Lynn, "that close."

The Ervins were thrilled that their son was receiving guidance from a man with Roger's values.

After getting fired by the Canucks, Neilson joined the Chicago Blackhawks as an assistant coach. He didn't see Todd much during the winter months, but he arranged to meet the Ervins during a Blackhawks road trip to Vancouver in late November, 1985.

Todd and his parents went to the game and met Roger afterward. In the scene outside the coaches' offices, Todd gave his mentor an especially big bear hug.

Back home, the Ervins were watching a replay of the B.C. Lions Grey Cup parade when they heard Todd fumbling around in the kitchen. Outside, a light snow was falling. Todd was asking about his asthma medication. He could feel a bad attack coming on.

"Mom, you better call an ambulance," he told Lynn.

"Okay, but can't I just drive you to the hospital?"

"Mom, if you don't call an ambulance, I'm not going to make it."

Todd's body was lapsing into anaphylactic shock. He died on the way to the hospital.

The Ervins called Roger at his hotel to tell him Todd had been rushed to emergency. Neilson took a taxi to the hospital, where he learned Todd was dead. The Ervins, and Roger, were devastated.

"What do you worry about as a parent?" says Lynn, then answered her own question: "Alcohol, drinking and driving, drugs."

Not asthma. Or the odds of dying from it.

Neilson took a leave from the Blackhawks and remained in Vancouver for a week, attending Todd's memorial and grieving with the Ervins and their friends.

"I've never loved anyone," Roger told Lynn and Nate, "like I loved your son."

Neilson returned to the Blackhawks, but his mind was far from hockey. So deep was his mental funk, his friends grew worried about his welfare.

Rob Campbell contacted Bob Pulford in Chicago to make sure Roger was okay.

"It was hard to see Rog in that frame of mind," says Devin Smith. "He couldn't snap out of it, wouldn't let it go. It would always be, 'I wish Todd was here, I wish Todd was here, I wish Todd was here,' every trip after that. . . .

"In my life of knowing him, it was the toughest time he went through. He's had so many friends, but none as close as Todd. He relied on Rog a lot. And he talked to him all the time.

"Todd was a really charismatic kid, he was unbelievable. He was the kind of kid that, when he died, you look back on it and say, 'There's a reason why he was who he was.' If you believe in fate, which I do. He probably knew he wasn't going to be here forever and made the most of every day."

Every day, for the rest of Roger's life, he paid homage to Todd Ervin. The first summer after the boy's death, Roger staged a week-long Todd Reunion for Todd's friends from Ontario to B.C. It was almost eerie, the artifacts Roger kept at his house. He kept Todd's Angels cap and his asthma inhaler on a small mantel, along with Todd's picture. A shrine of sorts.

On the last Christmas Todd celebrated, his father had given him a Mariner's Cross, a seaman's crucifix for safe passage, on a gold chain. Todd and Roger shared a love for boats and open water.

"Roger should have this," said Nate Ervin. Todd had become a Christian before he died, a development that provided Roger no small amount of comfort.

For the rest of his life, Roger wore Todd's chain around his neck. Those who were with him at the end say he spent his final days talking of Todd and clasping that chain and cross.

About twenty minutes after Roger died, Darren Keily called the Ervins to break the news.

Like Roger's many other friends, the Ervins spent a tough weekend, thinking about Roger – so much about Roger that

Lynn didn't make what would later seem an obvious connection.

"Four days after Roger died, I was back at work when I was overcome with this sense that Roger and Todd were at peace, because they were finally together," says Lynn. "It was the most comforting feeling. I thought, 'I don't need to grieve anymore.'

"The amazing thing was, five minutes later Nate came over from the other side of the building where we work, and he said, 'You know, I was just thinking, Roger and Todd are happy together now.'"

On the Road Again

Perhaps because his mother was from another continent and his father opened their door to visiting missionaries from far-off lands, Roger Neilson felt right at home when he was on the road.

Neilson's entire career in the NHL was nomadic, even by the standards of the transient professional-coaching business. He served as head coach of seven different franchises – eight, counting the two games he coached in Ottawa to push his games total to one thousand – and didn't stay in one NHL city as long as four seasons. The longest tenure he enjoyed in any hockey town was the ten years of junior hockey he spent in Peterborough.

In twenty-six professional seasons involving a range of coaching capacities, Neilson put down shallow roots in the NHL centres of Toronto, Buffalo, Vancouver, Los Angeles (briefly), Chicago,

Edmonton (even more briefly), New York, Florida, St. Louis, Philadelphia, and Ottawa.

So what did Roger do in his spare time? In between gigs?

The great gypsy travelled, of course, often leaving his agent, Rob Campbell, with these parting words: "Find me a job by the time I get back."

Roger listened to his mother talk of growing up in South Africa. His father had travelled in Europe and Africa.

"Roger was always craving knowledge," says Kent Pearce, a Neilson protegé, "learning something about the history of other places. He was a teacher. He always wanted to learn about new cultures and new people. And he had the means to do it."

Starting small, Roger was travelling long before he reached the NHL. As sure as the wheels were turning in his head ("his brain never stopped working," says friend and neighbour Ruby Bell), the wheels were turning on his beater Volkswagen van; amazing, really, considering that Neilson hated to drive, routinely fell asleep at the wheel, and constantly recruited fifteen- and sixteen-year-olds, some with licences, some without, to get behind the wheel. This was Roger the crazy uncle, who let the kids get away with things when a parent's head was turned.

"I remember he had a broken leg one time and I shifted gears for him, because all the cars were standard in those days," says Doug Peacock, one of Roger's minor hockey players in Toronto. "He got a big laugh out of things like that."

Roger was born with a spirit for adventure, ready at the drop of his ball cap to set off somewhere, sometimes as far as a tank of gas would get him. His earliest trips were by van and car, to baseball destinations within easy reach. On the spur of the moment, he took minor league ball teams to Tiger Stadium in Detroit and to World Series locales. It's easy to look back on those outings and imagine the spontaneous enthusiasm at the heart of them. "Hey, the Series is on! Let's go, gang!" And off they went, without a care for such

technicalities as where to stay or how to get into sold-out stadiums. With Roger, things always worked out; that is, if sleeping in jail cells in Schenectady, New York, can be called a reasonable solution to an accommodation issue.

Dick Todd, who pitched for Roger and was later his trainer with the Peterborough Petes, remembers going to New York with Roger and a gang of ball players for the 1960 World Series between the Pittsburgh Pirates and New York Yankees.

The group of eight, including Roger, swarmed the Bronx streets looking for tickets, quickly learning the nuances of the scalper trade. Todd got into one game for free, after buying and reselling tickets until his profits covered the cost of entry.

This was the World Series Bill Mazeroski would ultimately win with a swing of the bat in game seven at Pittsburgh, but Roger and his boys witnessed earlier games in what some have called the strangest World Series in history. Strange for the way in which the Yankees mashed in their three victories, winning by scores of 16-3, 10-0, and 12-0. Bobby Richardson had a huge Series for the Bombers; yet the Pirates eked out wins in the other four games to prevail.

"Four of the gang wanted Pittsburgh and the other four were Yankee fans," says Todd. "We had bets going back and forth."

They also had an older boy in their group, a pro prospect named Bobby McKillop, who had played some minor league ball for Roger. Through McKillop, Roger's boys were able to meet Pirate first baseman Rocky Nelson, a legendary slugger in the International League with the Toronto Maple Leafs. Nelson posed for pictures with Roger's kids on the turf of Yankee Stadium.

McKillop's parents were in town for the Series, and when they discovered Roger and his "orphans" had no place to stay, they insisted on sharing their hotel room, despite the inconvenience.

"We had cots and bunk beds stretched across every inch of that room," says Todd.

The boys didn't know how good they had it, until the ride home. A stickler for detail and preparation in baseball and hockey, Roger wasn't quite as thorough with his automobile maintenance. The old Volks van had no gas gauge, and half the time Roger didn't bother to refill the auxiliary tank he had on hand when the main tank ran dry. A more pressing issue was a generator working at about 30 per cent capacity. Trudging along a New York State freeway at about thirty miles an hour, the headlights giving off the soft glow of a fading flashlight, Neilson's van was a beacon for state troopers trying to solve a roadblock problem northwest of Albany.

Once the van was pulled aside and rested a little, it picked up some steam, but was soon dogging it again, now closely monitored by police. The cops helped Roger try to locate a hotel room for the night, but when nothing was available they suggested a final option. Spare cells at the town jail in Schenectady.

"There was a prisoner in one of the three jail cells, and we were in the other two," says Todd. "They didn't lock us in or anything, but in the middle of the night we heard this clanging going on. They'd brought in another customer, so we were down to one cell, and a few of the kids had to move out into a hallway, sleeping in sleeping bags on the concrete."

Roger took his kids on ball trips to Detroit, Cleveland, Baltimore, New York. They saw the colourful Jimmy Piersall run the bases backwards after hitting his thousandth career home run. They saw a fan run onto the field and make a circular motion with his forefinger to suggest Piersall was crazy. Piersall chased the fan all the way to the foul line, where he booted him in the rear end. Roger's boys howled with delight.

Piersall, troubled by mental illness, once said famously, "Probably the best thing that ever happened to me was going nuts."

Though baseball was the main course, Roger would always look for a side dish of amusement parks. He'd seek out the largest

roller coaster he could find and take the gang for a ride. Cleveland had a good one.

Sometimes the road trips were closer to home, but exhausting nonetheless for anyone without Roger's stock of energy. He bought a used, perhaps overused, Ford Galaxie in the mid 1960s and drove it on a back-and-forth triangular route from Toronto to Algonquin Park to Detroit on a single weekend. Seems the coach had plans to see a series at Tiger Stadium, but there was also the possibility of his boys having to compete in a Toronto little league tournament, and one of Roger's best pitchers was on a camping trip in Algonquin Park.

So, Roger drove the Galaxie 160 miles northeast to Algonquin to retrieve his pitcher, then tacked 400 miles southeast to Detroit for the Friday night Tigers' game. The next morning, they hustled back to Toronto, played a tournament game, and returned to Motor City for Sunday's matinee. When that was over, Roger – or more accurately, one or more of his teenage driver recruits – drove his pitcher back to Algonquin and brought the rest of the kids home to Toronto.

In the first month of the Galaxie's time with Roger, it had picked up an extra ten thousand miles on the odometer. Still not fully grasping an old car's oil needs, Roger saw his Galaxie seize up and die at the Highway 7 and 400 interchange northwest of Toronto. Like his dogs, Roger's car died a hero.

●

On another early tour, Roger took a few of his Toronto carriers and athletes to Arizona and California, down Route 66. They arrived at the Grand Canyon after dark but were too excited to wait for daylight, so they ventured down the trail to the bottom of the Canyon. After stumbling along for several hundred feet, three of the group bailed and went back up. Roger and the other

three carried on, catching the sound of rattlesnakes as they approached the Colorado River.

Hiking back up wasn't an option, so the group bedded down in the riverbed, warm in the natural shelter. Roger slept with a stick in his hand, just in case any of the rattlers came calling. Meanwhile, the poor group that stayed up top were half frozen in the desert night air. They slept on benches, unable to get into Roger's locked car because the driver had the keys in his pocket, a mile below.

The hikers woke up in the morning and had a swim in the Colorado River before walking back up. Eventually, they reached Huntington Beach, California, and saw America's first McDonald's restaurant.

Roger never tired of travelling with young adventurers. There was something in their wide-eyed wonder at new experiences, and he fed off their energy, which he matched or exceeded. They'd put headphones on him on an aircraft, crank up a little George Thorogood, and then giggle as Roger started to sing along, loud enough for everyone on the plane to hear. When his recruits grew older and had children of their own, he'd take their kids and leave the dads behind. Sometimes the old boys would bug him to let them go along. In the summer of 2002, Roger took a group of the old boys to Hawaii for a week – a week later, they flew back and the kids arrived in their place.

"He just was always driven," says Nancy Nichols. "If he was a child today, he'd probably be on Ritalin. Anybody who coaches that many teams and throws that many papers and sleeps four hours a day . . . he really was driven. I think a normal person would have died from his cancer within a year. He had this energy and drive that makes me tired just to talk about it."

The Roger tours ran the full gamut. He'd jet to Australia or Africa and breeze through regions at an astonishing rate.

"He never stopped and looked around to smell the coffee," says Nichols. "Eight years ago, he took some kids on a trip, went to twenty-one countries in twenty-two days. He visited Cape Town, went up through Africa. In three weeks, they went across Africa, Israel, Rome, Germany, Monaco, up to Paris, and missed a plane and ended up London."

"I'm an Africa freak," says Nichols. "A safari person. I spend two weeks in a camp, slowly tracking animals. Roger went all that way and went into the bush for an afternoon.

"Remember Chevy Chase in *National Lampoon's Family Vacation*? He goes to the Grand Canyon, says, 'Okay, take my picture, now let's go.' Well, that's how Roger did the world. And it's kind of how he did his life."

Al Dunford was teaching in Nigeria before Neilson and Dunford joined the Leafs staff in the late 1970s. In typical fashion, Ballard completely fabricated a tale of how he "just put a call through to Roger in Africa" to inform him he was being hired as the new head coach in Toronto. In fact, Ballard didn't speak to Neilson, who, according to Dunford, wasn't in Africa at the time but in Europe.

While Dunford was teaching in Africa, Neilson would correspond by audiotape. After his first professional season with the AHL Dallas Blackhawks, Neilson flew to Africa to meet up with Dunford and do some travelling. On Neilson's urging, Dunford was subsequently hired by the Leafs as travel secretary in Roger's second Leaf season.

Dunford's recollection of the worldly Neilson includes a complete fascination with Israel. They flew to Tel Aviv, via Rome, in early summer 1977.

"As a traveller, Roger was thoroughly organized and had a clear picture of what he wanted to do," says Dunford. "But it was a whirlwind. An 'if-it's-Tuesday-this-must-be-Belgium' kind of thing. He researched the history of Israel ahead of time, but he was

a manic traveller. He went at a breakneck speed through things."

In contrast to Neilson's whirlwind world travel were the regular junkets to Hawaii, where the joy was in ritual and tradition, repeating the same holiday pattern for sixteen years. It was essential to Roger that his group stay at the same condo, eat at the same restaurants, play the same golf courses, buy helicopter rides from the same operator.

In Maui, Roger always stayed at the Nohonani townhouse resort in Lahaina, Maui. Marga "Blue" Robinson was the sales manager. Roger loved that name, Blue Robinson. Blue was, and is, a great character in her own right. And she loved experiencing the Roger invasion every summer.

Blue keeps a Roger bobblehead doll on the counter and has pictures on the wall of Neilson's NHL teams.

Roy Mlakar, the Senators president and CEO, spent his honeymoon in Hawaii on the Roger Plan. Mlakar and his new bride, Tammy, left for Maui with a detailed set of instructions from Roger, everything from where to eat to where to buy tickets for recreational activities.

Devin Smith, a Roger Hawaii veteran, and his bride, Sue, also honeymooned in Maui. No slight to his bride, Smith said it felt weird to be there without Roger.

Roger could squeeze a dollar until it cried for help. That didn't mean an aversion to frills and the scams that made them possible. In Maui, Roger would sneak his group into the good hotels, act like paying guests, and enjoy the privileges of a swank pool and other facilities.

And not always with discretion. Forever eighteen, Roger loved to wrestle and fool around like one of the guys. They'd hack around in a swimming pool. At the Hyatt Hotel pool, the trespassers were pretending to drown each other when Smith held Roger's head under water and pushed him next to a seventy-year-old man minding his own business. Roger burst to the

surface, grabbed the man by the head thinking it was Smith, then backed away in embarrassment as the poor old fellow screamed in fear.

Far away, at the side of the pool, Smith looked on in mock innocence.

In trying to keep up with the kids, Neilson was forever getting hurt. His entourage considered it part of the entertainment package. They'd walk along a beachfront in Maui, see Roger heading straight for some protruding branches, but say nothing as he walked right into them. They'd laugh, he'd get mad, then retell the story to the rest of the group and make everyone howl.

His trips were devoted to appeasing the young travellers, having them experience the road to the fullest. Roger would rent mopeds, or scooters for the kids, and delight in the action as they raced around.

His stubbornness extended to recreational activities.

He was bugging Smith to go parasailing in Hawaii. Smith said he didn't want to. "You have to go," Roger said.

He went, and enjoyed it, but realized his participation was more important to Roger than to himself. "He liked to get up early and do things," says Smith. "It was always about making the best of the day and trying new things. 'Don't be sleeping your life away,' he'd say. And of course, we were teenagers and liked our sleep."

In 1993, after Roger was fired by the Rangers, Devin Smith and Kent Pearce accompanied Roger on a three-week tour of New Zealand and Australia. Roger's beloved dog Mike had just died. The timing was right to hit the road in a major way.

Pearce was playing Junior C hockey in Schomberg, north of Toronto, at the time, but Neilson didn't consider that an obstacle. When Pearce told his mother about Roger's offer, Susan Pearce quietly told Kent's coach, and the coach told Pearce with a smile, "You're benched for three weeks if you don't go."

Pearce went, and the troika wasn't in Sydney very long before Roger managed to find an old beater to rent. You could get Roger away from the routine, but there was no getting the old habits out of Roger.

The trip went smoothly, after Mr. Magoo nearly wiped out the mailbox.

They took in the view of the spectacular Sydney Harbour, from land and by boat. They drove to Melbourne and headed north to experience the Great Barrier Reef. As often happens on grand excursions, it was the simple pleasures the tourists remembered best. In New Zealand, the boys rented a car and drove from top to bottom of the country along a coastal highway, only stopping to play golf along the way. Most of the courses were quaint; one had a cement box near the first tee with a sign asking golfers to deposit twenty dollars for a round. It's safe to assume Roger, Pearce, and Smith were the only Canadian golfers using clubs they'd carted from home, halfway around the globe.

"Roger was so happy on that trip," says Smith. "We golfed every day, sometimes twice a day. Just threw the clubs in the back and drove."

The highlight of the trip was Roger's first bungee jump, which he seemed to sign on for without realizing what was involved. This was at Lake Taupo, in the heart of New Zealand's North Island. Roger paid up, including a little extra for the video (as if Captain V. could say no), and then blurted out to Pearce and Smith, "So, what exactly is this thing all about?"

Smith said, "Well, Rog, you strap that rubber band onto your leg and you jump to your death."

"Oh, okay," said Roger, who was looking forward to his fifty-ninth birthday in a few months.

Roger lived, but came to regret not wearing socks on his sandalled feet. The ankle rash from the bungee bothered him for

days. Otherwise, he surprised his young pals by the nonchalance with which he treated the experience.

"People usually have a big adrenaline rush after something like that," says Smith. "Roger's reaction was, 'So, do you want to go get some ice cream?'"

Though he might have been cool about it at the time, Roger was exceedingly proud of taking the plunge (without getting married) in New Zealand. Three years later, at age sixty-two, he jumped again at Victoria Falls in South Africa, a feat that had added significance because he was close to his mother's birthplace. "He bragged about that jump forever," says Nancy Nichols. "It was one of the most fun things he ever did, and he loved the fact he was in his sixties when he did it. If he had won a Stanley Cup, he would have been standing at Heaven's gate, saying, 'Hmmm, Stanley Cup . . . bungee jump . . . I'm not sure which was more important.'"

The long hockey season didn't entirely preclude travel for Roger's Boys. When Neilson was an assistant coach with the Chicago Blackhawks in the mid-eighties, he invited Devin and Landry Smith on a team road trip. They sat up front with the pilots, saw Boston Garden and met Terry O'Reilly, then a rookie head coach with the Bruins.

"Everything was always first class," says Smith, "and there was always something funny that happened."

He kept tabs on his protégés and made up excuses to see them in person. While with the Rangers, Neilson called Kent Pearce, then a high school student, and told him he needed a videotape of the Leaf game on the Thursday night. Pearce had a hockey game that night, so his dad, Tom, taped the game. Roger got the Rangers to arrange Kent's flight from Toronto to Chicago, where the Rangers were playing that weekend.

"Obviously, he could have found other ways to get that tape," says Pearce. "He just wanted to fly me out to Chicago for the

weekend. He did things like that all the time. It's almost like he had little projects with a lot of us."

SETTING UP CAMP IN ISRAEL

He heard bomb blasts, daily, and felt a two-by-four fly past him, but it was the smiles on young faces that Roger Neilson remembered best of his time in Israel.

Marshall Starkman, manager of camp operations for Neilson's annual residential hockey school in Lindsay, Ontario, was visiting Israel in the mid-1990s when Starkman and Jeff Budd, volunteer co-ordinator of the Canada Centre in Metulla, Northern Israel, first kicked around the idea of an Israeli hockey camp.

Budd's job, in the plan, was to round up support and sponsorship money in Israel.

Marshall's assignment was to sell Roger, with his camp know-how, on the idea of taking his act on the road to Damascus, so to speak.

It was an easy job. Starkman knew of Neilson's affinity for Jerusalem, the centre of world religion.

"Yeah, that sounds like it could be good," said Neilson when Starkman approached him with the idea.

Now, *Hockey Night in Israel* isn't exactly endemic to the region. The sport is foreign to Israelis, and the climate doesn't lend itself to the backyard rink phenomenon. In fact, the nation has one hockey rink facility. Not coincidentally, it is at the Canada Centre, a double-rink athletic complex that owes its life to donations made by Canadians, mostly from Jewish groups in cities like Winnipeg and Montreal.

Initially, the lone skating rink was a miniature facility about half the size of a North American ice surface. In the early nineties, an attractive Olympic-size rink was built, even if it had some quirks that would make a Canadian hockey player giggle. For example, the arena Plexiglas would routinely pop out from the

impact of a body check, and it would take up to three weeks to get a replacement piece. Along the inside of the boards was a handrail running completely around the rink, to help prop up beginner skaters. It boggles the mind to think what NHL players could do to opponents with the opportunity to slam them into that.

Metulla is a residential town on the Israel–Lebanon border, a Middle East political hot spot and a frequent target of guerrilla bombing. These are circumstances not easily hidden, even from the less-than-worldly members of the NHL Players' Association.

In the inaugural year, 1997, Roger was scheduled to bring Dallas Eakins and Bill Lindsay as his two professionals, along with Starkman and Roger's chief camp instructor, Alex Andjelic. But Eakins was scared off by news of a bus bombing in the area and pulled out of the trip. That left a very nervous Bill Lindsay. Organizers did their best to hide from Lindsay the news that Eakins had bailed – and when he did find out, they did their best to deflect his concerns.

Days before he was supposed to depart, Lindsay was wavering badly on the phone with Starkman. So Starkman called in reinforcements. Ellie Rubenstein of the United Israel Appeal talked to Bill and laid a heavy guilt trip on him, reminding him this was the launch year for Hockey Project Israel, that the kids were expecting NHL pros, and that Lindsay was the only pro left on the marquee. Rubenstein promised Bill he would have a great time, that his life would not be in danger. Ultimately, Lindsay relented. And only temporarily did he regret that decision.

Starkman remembers seeing Lindsay before departure at the airport, looking sad, annoyed, wearing a face that said, "I can't believe you guys have done this to me."

Miraculously – maybe it was the in-flight service – somewhere over the ocean Lindsay came to accept his fate. He was right into the hockey missionary business by the time they arrived in Israel.

Days later, he wasn't so sure. There'd been an attack in southern Lebanon, creating the expectation of retaliation. News crews, including CNN, were pouring into the hotel where Neilson's staff were housed.

Lindsay was beside himself. He took what he saw as the only reasonable measure: he asked the night watchman if he could please open up the hotel bar so that a frightened man could get a drink. "If we're going out, we're going out in style," he said. A day later, the tensions had settled, and Lindsay lived to return to North America and his NHL job.

In Year Two of Roger's Israel camps, Dainius Zubrus, then coming off his rookie year with Philadelphia, was one of the pros. At nineteen, the Russian forward was younger than some of the kids on the ice. And he, too, was petrified of the conflict going on around him. The camp staffers used to joke that Zubrus slept under the bed, like a puppy in a thunderstorm, the whole time he was in Israel. The Zubrus stories were good comic relief, funny in retrospect because none of the barnstorming hockey gang was hurt during their visit.

The third year of Roger's desert hockey phase, Steve Dubinsky, a member of the Calgary Flames at the time, was part of the entourage. The trip was especially meaningful for Dubinsky and his wife, Cheryl, because they are Jewish.

All things considered, the timing of the camp in Metulla was almost ideal. For the first time, hockey had been included in the fifteenth World Maccabiah Games in July of 1997, just a month before Neilson's troops arrived, armed with hockey sticks, pucks, and hundreds of years of combined hockey experience.

Until then, a keen local coach, a Russian emigrant named Boris Mendel, was the source of nearly all hockey knowledge in Israel. Mendel was thrilled to have his efforts boosted by the arrival of Neilson with his NHL background. The campers ranged in age from seven or eight up to seventeen and eighteen, older than

a typical North American summer camp, because for many Israeli teenagers it was their first taste of hockey. For some children, it was the highlight of their year. They listened attentively when Roger spoke, occasionally using a bit of the Hebrew he'd acquired. They smothered him with hugs. Gritty, determined, if not exactly smooth on their skates, they participated in scrimmages with the zeal and passion of players in a championship final. One of the older, more skilled campers was invited to join a Dutch club team, an arrangement made by Andjelic.

"They were so glad to have people come over," says Starkman. "They understood the meaning behind someone in the NHL volunteering his time to come over and work with them. Maybe they didn't know Bill Lindsay, because they didn't see a lot of NHL coverage, but they knew he was a pro player."

After coaching Canadian kids who experience so much (maybe too much) so young in hockey, Neilson was taken aback by the demeanour of the Israeli players. They would thank their instructors after every training session, every game. Most of the children hadn't seen an NHL game before. Roger mailed them videotaped games when he got back home.

"These kids love hockey," Roger told a Toronto journalist. "It's 40 degrees outside and they just want to put on their gear and get on the ice."

"You could never top that first year," says Starkman, "even though the camp grew and we added all kinds of fun things, you couldn't beat the first year because of the process of getting it off the ground. Getting there – and the overwhelming feeling of warmth. They really laid the red carpet out for us."

Roger connected with one particular Israeli boy and stayed in touch with him and his family by mail. And just like that, Roger's Boys had their first overseas chapter.

What started as a casual camp of fewer than forty skaters grew each summer until there were about a hundred participants

in the 2000 camp. Hockey interest spilled over into local minor hockey registrations, which doubled after Roger's initial foray into Metulla.

In his later years, Roger didn't make many on-ice appearances at his Canadian camp, leaving the skating to the younger instructors. But in Israel, with a smaller staff, he ran practices day and night. He went behind the bench and worked closely with this keen, curious, quick-study group.

Home or away, there was an aura around Roger Neilson. Starkman speaks of the thrill being able to work alongside him on the ice and behind the bench at the Canada Centre facility.

The camps were structured to allow time for staff and campers – some from North America – to tour Jerusalem and the surrounding countryside. In Year One of what would become a four-year program, Roger took a group to a bomb shelter, which was loaded with families who had occupied it as a routine precaution.

"It took Roger about five minutes to spark up a ping-pong tournament with the kids," says Starkman.

The visitors learned a rule of thumb about the sound of bomb shells. If it's loud, relax, the shell is outgoing. If it's muffled, followed by a pop, start worrying, because it's incoming. (And Roger learned to keep his eyes open, after nearly getting clubbed by a wooden board thrown by a child in the Old City of Jerusalem.)

Roger and his staff grew to accept the fact that they would hear bombs in the background even as they sat by the hotel pool. It was here that Roger had his impromptu meeting with the Israeli president of the day, Ezer Weizman.

With his deep religious faith and a background of education and travel, Neilson had a strong appreciation and knowledge of Israel. He could easily have stepped in for the tour guides on the buses they took to the tourist sites. He would provide background

for the visiting pros about a particular relic or important battle – and he knew a lot about Weizman and his history as a fighter pilot.

When there was serious shelling in a particular area of the country, it was usual for a dignitary to make a goodwill visit to boost spirits and check on the locals and important visitors. At the Canada Centre, Jeff Budd received a call saying that the president was dropping by on a moment's notice. Budd called Starkman at the hotel and suggested he round up the camp staff to meet the prez at the rink in about ten minutes.

Neilson was running an errand at the time, so Starkman and Andjelic, sitting poolside, hot-footed off together. In Andjelic's case, this was literally true. He didn't bother to stop and get his shoes, a move he regretted as he burned the soles of his feet on the hot Israeli asphalt.

Starkman managed to remember his camera, but was scared stiff by the armed security around the president. Alex implored Starkman to get a picture, then shook Weizman's hand for about a minute, stalling while Starkman tried to work up his courage.

"I'm worried the flash is going to off and all these guys are going to tackle me or shoot me," says Starkman. "So I didn't take the picture. Later, Jeff said it wouldn't have been a problem. Alex was mad at me for the longest time. 'Nobody is ever going to believe I met the president of Israel,' he grumbled."

Back at the hotel, Roger was at the pool, getting a good laugh as the story was retold. At that very moment, a motorcade pulled into the hotel entrance area and in walked the president. Starkman brought Roger over to meet him.

This was Roger unplugged. Barefoot. Wearing a bathing suit, T-shirt, and ball cap over his shaggy curls. Tanned to the colour and texture of a shortstop's mitt. He smiled broadly as he shook President Weizman's hand, and this time Starkman stepped up and recorded the moment on film.

"You already look 102 per cent Israeli," Weizman told Roger, who looked for all the world like an aging kibbutznik.

The North American contingent usually spent a day and half in Jerusalem after arriving, and another day and half in Tel Aviv at the end of the camp. The Old City, the Dead Sea, and the Masada ruins in the Judea Desert were must-see components in Roger's annual tour of Israel. Toronto journalist Lisi Tesher was with the group in August of 2000, which turned out to be the final year for the Neilson camp in Israel. As they hiked in the desert, Tesher remembers their guide cautioning the group, many with bare arms and shoulders, about the sun's harmful rays. "You could get cancer," said the guide. "Be careful."

"I already have cancer," said Roger, unable to contain himself. "I've got nothing to worry about."

Just five months later, Neilson did have a new worry. He was diagnosed with a second cancer, malignant melanoma.

At the eleventh hour of that fourth Neilson camp in Metulla, staff told the twenty to twenty-five North American children planning on attending not to come. The Israeli troops had pulled out of Southern Lebanon, so there was no longer a buffer zone between Metulla and Lebanon. Concerned enough about the uncertainties, the administrators of Roger's camp advised the North American families it was too unsafe.

A year later, it wasn't safe for any of the camp staff to go back to this northern Israeli outpost. Besides, Neilson had that second cancer to confront.

CHAPTER 8

Icing on the Career

His preference, as always, was to be the head coach, not an assistant.

So imagine Roger Neilson's surprise to find joy, peace, and lasting fame with the Ottawa Senators as a lieutenant to Jacques Martin for the final years of his NHL career, the final years of his life. The denouement he fought like hell to prolong.

For a time, after being terminated by the Philadelphia Flyers, Neilson wondered if he would work again at the NHL level. He had applied and been passed up for head coaching positions with the two expansion clubs, the Columbus Blue Jackets and the Minnesota Wild. The rebuilding Calgary Flames had also declined his services. So had the Tampa Bay Lightning, where he tried to catch on as an assistant.

Not that he blamed any organization for opting for someone else. Someone younger, healthier. "There's not a big demand," he liked to say, "for sixty-six-year-old cancer patients."

Neilson figured he could pick up some work in the fall as a television analyst. Physically, he felt good. His multiple myeloma was in remission and, ever optimistic, he was telling people the cancer wouldn't be an issue for another four or five years. In his wrier moments, he joked about coaching the junior team he owned, the Lindsay Muskies. Couldn't beat the convenience – a short drive away from his Chemong Lake home – and there weren't any millionaire players on the roster to give him grief.

But in the summer of 2000, Jacques Martin called from Ottawa to offer him the assistant's job that became available when André Savard left the Senators to become the director of player personnel with the Montreal Canadiens. All those coaching prospects Neilson had mentored from his early days with the Peterborough Petes were paying bonus dividends now. Martin was one of several NHL coaches to have been nurtured by Roger in some way, somewhere along the line. In Martin's case, he had stayed at Neilson's house while he was first finding his way in the game, having abandoned a teaching career to coach full time – first in the Central Junior Hockey League, then as an assistant to Dick Todd in Peterborough starting in 1984.

Martin worked his way up through the ranks in the OHL, winning a Memorial Cup championship with Guelph in 1985-86, which was his ticket to the NHL. After being hired by then–general manager Pierre Gauthier in Ottawa in January 1996, Martin had transformed the Senators from expansion laughingstock into a playoff contender. Under normal circumstances, Martin would have replaced Savard with another ex-player – the Senators had no other former NHLers on staff at the time – but Martin felt Neilson's experience and encyclopedic hockey mind would hold sway with his players.

Hiring Neilson turned out to be a stroke of genius. Other than the pain of seeing his health fade during his third and final Ottawa season, there was no downside to having Neilson on staff. Roger was the hockey legend in residence. His illness moved everyone to reflect on all that he had done for the game and to cherish his last valiant shot at a championship. Neilson and the Senators franchise, which embraced him without reservation, shared equally in the glow that was the twilight of Roger's career.

Martin enjoyed the benefit of the most battle-tested sounding board in all of hockey. Roger was a brainier version of Don Zimmer, the former dugout baseball resource of New York Yankees manager Joe Torre. There was nothing Neilson hadn't encountered in half a century of coaching and scouting. No rule he hadn't challenged or twisted. Along with his coaching influence, he was the travel secretary's best friend with his knowledge of every road hotel and the full gamut of logistical nuances away from home.

The Senators would turn out to be the answer to Roger's prayers, or maybe the reward for all his penance.

"I would use the word karma," says Roger's companion, Nancy Nichols, "but he would call it Jesus. It's like what he went through in Philadelphia got him Ottawa."

Ottawa was an oasis at the end of a long, hard trail. He could do no wrong in the Nation's Capital from the day he arrived. Fans adored him. Many still remembered him as the likeable foil in Harold Ballard's Byzantine operation at Maple Leaf Gardens. (The Ottawa Valley, remember, remained a Leaf stronghold even after the arrival of the Senators.) The media relished his dry wit, his one-liners. Like everyone else, they enjoyed the antics and the tales of Roger Neilson. There was no one else like him in the game.

As an assistant, Neilson had few of the pressures and media demands that are placed on a head coach, although visiting reporters still sought him out, many of them more concerned about his health than any particular story. Neilson focused on teaching, as

he had in St. Louis, Chicago, and Vancouver, working in a position that complemented the efforts of Martin's long-time assistant Perry Pearn. Players, staff, everyone would learn from a coach who had been in the NHL twice as long as the Ottawa franchise. Away from the rink, Roger engaged in his usual activities, bike and car mishaps and other misadventures he would share with his friends for a laugh at his own expense.

He spent much of his free time with Perry Pearn and Roy Mlakar, the team's CEO and president. They would share what Mlakar called Loser Sunday. This was in Roger's first couple of years in Ottawa, before Mlakar got married and before Perry's wife moved east for the hockey season.

Loser Sunday began with church. Then brunch.

"If we went to the Ritz Restaurant on the canal, I paid; if it was Denny's at the Centrum Plaza, Rog would pay," says Mlakar. "He was the world's biggest cheapskate – and most generous donor."

Rog was living in the Kanata apartment owned by Mike Eastwood, but regularly visited Mlakar and Pearn at the house they shared before Mlakar married former L.A. Lakers executive Tamera Vogel.

"He would walk in, ask, 'What's for dinner,' never bring anything, then sit there with the clicker and watch a hockey game or the Jays game," says Mlakar.

Neilson was a huge Jays fan. He especially liked third baseman Eric Hinske and predicted big things for starter Roy Halladay long before he started to win consistently. Neilson didn't quite live long enough to see Halladay win his first Cy Young Award.

"Want a glass of wine?" Mlakar would ask Roger.

"Sure."

"But he didn't really drink, so he would take one sip, leave it, and have ginger ale with dinner," says Mlakar. "After dinner, he might take a second sip of wine, say, 'See ya,' and then Perry would

watch out the window to see what he backed into on his way out, whether it was a car or tree."

Neilson would make sizeable contributions, some more subtle than others, to a young Ottawa franchise that was about to enjoy its first real successes after rejoining the NHL as an expansion club in 1992.

The players were drawn to his easy manner. He was a teacher, foremost, and in his first season with the Senators was still well enough to go on the ice most days. Players trusted him, could talk to him about anything, whether it was something related to the game or something personal in their lives.

He paid attention to their troubles, their challenges, and the players responded in kind. In the fall of 2001, after Neilson had been away receiving chemotherapy treatments, he was finally ready to make his first on-ice practice appearance of the season. Staff brought a red Senators carpet onto the ice and Daniel Alfredsson and Radek Bonk lined up for a mock ceremonial faceoff before practice. After Alfredsson won the draw, he gave the puck to a grinning Neilson and the players banged their sticks to the ice in tribute.

Randy Lee, the Senators conditioning coach and former video specialist, savoured every minute he spent with Neilson and looked up to him as a mentor and invaluable hockey resource. Lee is honest, upfront himself, and so appreciated those qualities in Neilson.

"He was so genuine, really cared about the players as people," says Lee. "Rog wasn't part of the business. He didn't like the business side of hockey, the money side. He didn't care if a guy was making three million dollars a year. He treated it like the old days, when it was just a team of twenty guys, all with important roles to play. There were no mind games with him. No manipulation."

It didn't escape Lee that the Senators players were hardly the only ones to connect with Roger. Every opponent, home or away, had a collection of players, coaches, trainers who turned to Neilson when he was in town.

"People flocked to him," says Lee, "with that look in their eye that they just *had* to see Rog. The impact that he had was phenomenal. He would talk to them for fifteen, twenty minutes."

Behind the scenes, Neilson provided input outsiders never knew about. Little things would crop up, situational matters, like opposition tendencies or faceoff alignments. If Neilson didn't have the automatic solution, he would think about it a while and then return with an answer. "He would always figure out a way," says Lee. "And it was stuff you wouldn't find in a coach's manual. It might be some obscure little wrinkle that he remembered from ten years ago."

In his spare time, though, Neilson found himself blushing at unexpected honours, scribbling out notes for one thank-you address after the other. On the afternoon of a tribute dinner for Roger in Toronto – three days past his sixty-eighth birthday, came the announcement that would send a buzz through Roger's world. Neilson received a call informing him he was being inducted into the Hockey Hall of Fame.

"It's kind of magical," said Neilson, "the way things are happening these days."

For the occasion, he splurged and bought a spotted bow tie from upmarket clothier Harry Rosen, as wild an item as a guy can find at such a classy establishment. He couldn't have been in better form. "Doctors told me I should watch Leafs games to avoid excitement," said Roger, glancing from the podium to find the Leafs coach Pat Quinn. "Good one, eh, Pat?"

The occasion wasn't all barbs and chuckles. Writing in the *National Post,* Cam Cole captured the poignancy of Neilson's presence at the game between the Canadiens and Maple Leafs that preceded the inductions.

When the Hall's four new members – Neilson, St. Louis scoring whiz Bernie Federko, menacing winger Clark Gillies of

the Islanders' dynasty and the Washington Capitals' classic stay-at-home defenceman, Rod Langway – were introduced at Air Canada Centre on Saturday night, the ovation for Neilson was the kind that makes neck hair stand on end.

On and on it went, as Neilson, making bashful eye contact with the legends who lined the carpet applauding him, choked back tears that would have taken far too long to explain. Then, just before the ceremonial faceoff, he and fellow cancer survivor Saku Koivu, the Montreal Canadiens captain, shook hands, and an unmistakable look of shared triumph, and support, and hope, passed between them.

That was a moment so real, it could never have been staged.

"When I was out there on the ice, I kind of wondered what I was doing out there and whether I deserved all these honours," Neilson said. "But I think people realize, just like they did with Saku, that you're fighting a battle and they want to show they're on your side. I think it's nice that people feel that way."

The subject of Neilson putting up his feet for a while arose. Surely he'd earned the rest, could maybe use the rest. Roger implied that he preferred to die with his boots on. "I've looked at retirement and I just can't see myself retiring," he said. "It's not like I have a lot of grandchildren to go and see. I'd be able to get another dog."

Magic was in the air throughout his Ottawa stay. Remarkable things would happen. For example, here was a coach who arrived in town with a resume that clearly showed 973 games as an NHL head coach. It was right there in the Senators 2000-01 media guide. Then the media relations staff of the Senators – Phil Legault, Steve Keogh, and Ian Mendes – uncovered a discrepancy in Jacques Martin's coaching totals. That got them checking the coaching totals of all their staff, and they discovered the NHL's

data had Neilson with 998 games as a head coach. The Senators contacted the NHL and were informed that Roger was credited with the twenty-five games in Philadelphia coached by assistant Craig Ramsay while Neilson was recuperating from his stem-cell transplant surgery.

One minute a guy is sitting there minding his own business, breaking down game film. Next thing he knows he's picked up twenty-five games, sixteen of them victories, without breaking a sweat. How beautiful is life, that Neilson would get credit for those games in Philadelphia he felt should have been his to coach? After all his years of quiet, devoted faith, one could imagine him sitting in Ottawa thinking, "Yes, there is a God." Now he'd have ammunition the next time he was telling kids about the rewards of clean living.

The additional games elevated Neilson agonizingly close to a big, round milestone. The Senators PR department informed general manager Marshall Johnston, and he and Mlakar hatched the idea of Neilson stepping behind the Senators bench for a couple of games as head coach to reach the one thousand plateau. They waited until the Senators had qualified for a playoff position, then approached Martin about the idea of stepping aside for the final two games of the 2001-02 regular season. The scheduled opponents, Boston and Toronto, had both qualified for the play-offs, so there would be no issue of Ottawa's bench change altering the playoff picture. Johnston cleared the move with the NHL and declared the approval a "slam dunk."

Martin, a man of class and taste who happens to be Neilson's sartorial opposite, gracefully agreed. He understood.

Neilson was overwhelmed. He could now claim, if he wanted, to have been a head coach with eight different NHL teams, more than anyone else.

There is, of course, a dubious aspect to that sort of transience, which Neilson was only too glad to point out. "Usually this big a

crowd means I'm getting fired," he told an unusually large group of reporters after the announcement was made. "So at least that has changed. This was a complete surprise, but it's typical of the Senators organization, so perhaps it wasn't unexpected.

"If Harold Ballard ever figured that I'd be around for a thousand games, I'm sure he'd be rolling in his grave. Even the NHL phoned and warned me not to throw any sticks or water bottles."

And so Neilson ran the bench for games 81 and 82 of the season, two home games to the Bruins and Maple Leafs.

After winning game number 999 4-0, Neilson downplayed his role in his usual self-effacing manner, spiced with a little wicked humour.

"In the first period, I was kind of rusty," he said. "After that, it was pretty good. It wasn't a hard game to coach. Just turn the lines over. I don't know why they pay Jacques so much money."

Though he blushed slightly at all the attention, Neilson soaked up the tributes at the Corel Centre on what would be his last game as an NHL head coach. A capacity crowd waved white towels. Fans wore crazy Roger ties, and if they spilled any coke or pizza sauce on them, who would notice? Meanwhile, the scoreboard screen saluted Roger's NHL career, from paper bag to gatorade bottle toss to the famous journey to the Cup final with the Canucks.

In the press box, Harry Neale told the *Hockey Night in Canada* audience, "Two of the best things to happen in hockey for a long time: Koivu in Montreal and Neilson in Ottawa." Just days earlier, Saku Koivu had made a dramatic return from cancer treatment to rejoin his Canadiens teammates as they clinched a playoff berth. Now, here was Neilson, finishing up his career as head coach against the team that had launched it twenty-five years earlier: the Toronto Maple Leafs. It gave Roger pause to imagine himself among the legends of the game.

"Scotty [Bowman] and [Al] Arbour have incredible records in this league, but, when I was a kid, guys like Dick Irvin and Billy

Reay were big names," Neilson said. "So to be up there with them is a big thrill."

Irvin coached 1,449 NHL games, mostly with Montreal. Reay had 1,102, almost all with Chicago. In a manner of speaking, the Neilson ratings were in "grand" company.

The Leafs won that night, but the truth was that Neilson, as competitive as ever, treated the game, and the one before it, as though they were a test of the twenty-five years he'd spent warming up to that moment. When his Peterborough cronies came to visit him afterwards, Roger quickly assured them he hadn't missed a line matchup all night.

Same old Roger. Still looking for an edge.

The game officials presented Neilson with greeting cards when it was over, a nice change from the days when Roger used to abuse them.

Referee Kerry Fraser, knowing of Roger's affinity for canines, skated over to Roger and said, "Your dog would be proud."

One thousand games. Privately, Neilson hoped his health might improve to the point that he got a chance to add to the total.

"I've always said that, when it gets to be a drag to come in in the morning, I will know I've had enough," he said. "But it hasn't been like that at all. It's still as exciting as ever, breaking down the game before and getting ready for the next one."

Now, the race was on for Roger to achieve the one honour in hockey that had eluded him since he took on the Maple Leafs job twenty-six years earlier. Getting his name inscribed on the Stanley Cup. The 2002-03 Ottawa Senators had the look of a team that might get it done. Though Roger's health was slipping, he fought on, like a player who refused to be put on the disabled list at

playoff time. Hockey teams are famously evasive about the nature of injuries in the post-season, sending out descriptions of "upper" or "lower" body injuries. Neilson's body was hurting all over, and had been for some time. If Ottawa players needed any extra motivation, he provided the best possible example of dedication to the cause. Just getting to the arena was a major effort some days.

With winter setting in around the Corel Centre, Neilson's cancer had spread to the brain. On December 14, he received treatment for four separate brain tumours, which required the surgeons to drill holes in his skull. One can imagine the doctor telling Neilson to go home and rest after such a procedure. But it was a game night, and brain surgery wasn't going to keep Roger from going to work.

As he sat in the coach's booth, nodding in the direction of the press row during the national anthems before a game with the New Jersey Devils, his neon necktie shone even more brightly than usual below his pale complexion. Senators players marvelled at his will. They thought *they* were tough, sliding in front of slapshots and getting creamed into the boards. This was a different level of toughness. It left them humbled.

"He's been through more than I'd even want to think about facing," said defenceman Wade Redden, "but you never hear him feeling sorry for himself."

The goals Roger used to set for himself and for his teams, he now applied to his cancer. And so while he tried to build up strength by skipping road trips in the second half of the season, he was determined to get on that first charter flight of the playoffs. And he was on it. The fact that it was a successful playoff venture into Philadelphia, with his history there, made it all the more rewarding.

In his final Ottawa season, Roger's coaching role with the Senators changed. Pearn was looking after the power play duty that Neilson had the year before. And Don Jackson, a former NHL

defenceman, was on staff to look after defence and penalty killing. It left less of a gap when Roger was too sick to work or had to restrict his travel. He performed what teams call "pre-scout" work, analyzing an upcoming opponent and breaking down the appropriate game film.

Even in a lesser role, Neilson took pressure off Jacques Martin and represented a change of pace for the players. On game day afternoons, he would brief the players on what to look for from, say, the Flyers forwards, always knowing when to be funny and when to be serious.

Neilson was one of the few people who had Martin's ear. He could say things, suggest ideas, that even general manager John Muckler could not. As required, Roger could also take on the role of court jester.

In that same 2002-03 season, the Senators went through a horrible slump in late October and early November. They'd won just twice in their previous eight games and were coming home off a 7-1 drubbing by the Bruins that was nothing short of a Boston Massacre. Headlines were ugly.

Players were beaten up in more ways than one. A large crop of them was filing into the trainer's room for treatment before the morning skate, which had the makings of a gruelling workout known in the trade as a bag skate.

When trainer Gerry Townend's treatment room was about as full as it was going to get, in walked Neilson, wearing a straight face and his usual track suit.

"Gerry," he said, "I don't know what it is, but ever since I've been on this new medication, my dong keeps getting bigger."

And then Roger dropped his pants. Players were laughing so hard they almost peed themselves. They were still grinning as they walked out onto the ice for practice.

It was a well-needed laugh. Whether coincidentally or not, after Roger dropped his drawers, the Senators didn't drop a game

for the rest of the month, a ten-game undefeated streak on the way to a Presidents' Trophy.

●

The pace of an NHL schedule can wear out a healthy man. Three, sometimes four games a week, heavy practice schedules, game preparation, and forty-one dates on the road. For a sick man, battling two aggressive, incurable cancers while declining home nursing care, it's almost beyond comprehension. But this is the course Roger Neilson set out for himself. In the last half of the 2002-03 season, with his closest friends pleading with him to accept visits by a health nurse, Neilson resisted, insisting that twenty-three-year-old Nate Bedford, one of his hockey school goaltending counsellors from Peterborough, could look after him.

Nate, son of Neilson's camp director, Paul Bedford, was a renowned partier but a young man Neilson was extremely fond of and determined to make into a success story. It was a work-in-progress.

Bedford tells me of the time when he was seventeen and looking after Neilson's house while Roger was in Israel for his late-summer hockey camp. Nate had been at a friend's, partying all night, and went to bed at about 6:00 a.m. When he left a couple of hours later to go home, eight or nine other people asked him to drop them off on the way. He was driving Neilson's Suburban truck, wasn't as sober as he imagined, and passed out while driving on a dirt road. The truck flipped over onto its roof and six of the occupants had to be taken to hospital.

"It was not a real fond moment for me," says Bedford.

Neilson came home from the trip, briefly scolded Nate for being so irresponsible, then never raised the subject again.

"He took me with him when he picked up a new Suburban," says Bedford. "He flipped me the keys and let me drive it home."

So when Roger phoned in the fall of 2002, sick and in need of care, Nate Bedford happily answered the call.

As Neilson's health grew worse in December and into the New Year, many of Roger's closest friends, in the Senators organization and in the NHL, pleaded with him to take on some professional health care beyond the outstanding medical treatment he was receiving from doctors in Ottawa and Philadelphia. His friends also worked on Bedford to convince Roger to get some home care, but Nate, like Roger, dug in his heels.

"There's a lot of negativity toward me sometimes, which is understandable," says Bedford. "Someone that important, and you have a twenty-three-year-old looking after you. You want the best care for Roger Neilson, and in his mind that probably *was* the best care."

When he was at the rink, Roger was leaning on his colleagues in a way he hadn't at any other time in his career.

"I'm on borrowed time, here," he told Randy Lee one day. "You gotta help me out, here."

One night, when a home game was heading into overtime, up in the coach's booth Neilson was in distress and asking Lee if he thought the Senators could end it quickly in the extra period. Lee assured him they could.

Roger was shivering, taking pills, wrapped in blankets to try to keep warm. His illness affected his vision. There were nights when he couldn't see the ice down below.

Pearn and Tammy Mlakar did Roger's laundry, often soiled with blood. This was Roger's call, to keep working, but it took a team effort to carry it out.

Says Lee: "We were watching him die right before our eyes."

In their dark moments, the Senators preferred to remember the happier scenes, like the time in Florida when Roger was standing in his underwear after a shower, holding up two black spray cans. One was deodorant, the other hair spray.

"Hey, which one is which?" said Neilson.

Of course, he had already sprayed deodorant on his head and the hair spray under his arms. The sticky spray acted like velcro on his underarm hair. He couldn't lift his arms, it was so gooey.

"He really was like Mr. Magoo," says Lee.

As goofy as he could be, Neilson wanted to win as badly as anyone. He'd seen it all in nearly three decades of NHL employment, all except a Stanley Cup dance involving his team. In the Eastern Conference final of 2003, though Roger was deathly frail, unsteady as a newborn deer, he wanted his Senators players, some of them young and naive, to understand just how close this team was to achieving a lifetime moment.

In a sense, they did, because for the rest of their lives, Senators players will remember Roger's address before game five. Ottawa trailed the New Jersey Devils three games to one and was facing elimination on home ice. A season of promise for a Presidents' Trophy winner was slipping away, and yet a berth in the Stanley Cup was also just three victories away. The season was in the balance.

Roger Neilson was so sick he could barely watch the games. Working, helping out the team in his usual way, was out of the question. Still, the wheels were turning in that agile mind. There had to be something he could do – even if it was just a word of inspiration before a game of such importance.

Like kids to their daily classroom, the Senators filed into the video room, across the hall from their dressing room, for their usual pre-game instruction. They expected some last-minute reminders about keeping play simple against the methodical Devils.

And in walked this shadow of a man in the telltale track suit and ball cap. A man familiar and not familiar any more. It was all Roger could do to summon the physical strength to walk into that room, sit on the edge of a table, and speak to those young men before their big game. He did what he was asking the players to do – he dug deep.

Part of him opposed this tactic. He didn't want this to be the pleading speech of a dying man. The Gipper cliché. But he did want these players before him to understand how close they were and how fleeting the chance might be.

Privately, he was also worried about slipping up. As weak as he was physically, Roger was also in a variable state mentally. The cancer in his brain had tampered with the mind that was once the quickest in hockey. This was a critical address. He couldn't mess up. It would be brief.

"I've been in the NHL for twenty-six years and I've been with ten different teams and reached the finals once," said Roger, his weak voice carrying in the silent room.

He spoke to them about second chances. About enjoying the moment. Seizing the moment.

Implied, but not spoken, was the critical state on two fronts: Roger's life and the team's playoff life.

Roger walked out the door, exhausted by the effort he had just made, and was driven home to watch game five on TV.

When they regained their voices, and in some cases dried their eyes, the players and coaches of the Senators left the video room and made Roger proud in a 3-1 victory, after a tough start to the first period.

"Sometimes in hockey," says veteran centre Shaun Van Allen, "you can try too hard and not accomplish anything." But the Senators settled into their game and lit up a Corel Centre crowd suddenly taken with hope about a series comeback.

Van Allen, who knows about second chances in a hockey career, was still struck by Roger's words a year after the fact. "It was unbelievable. He was so weak, yet he wanted to do anything he could to try to help out the team."

The Senators did come back in the series. They beat the Devils in games five and six, stunning New Jersey with an overtime goal by Phillips at Continental Airlines Arena to bring the series home

for the finale. Everything was in place for the storybook ending that would send Roger and the Senators to the Cup final against the Anaheim Mighty Ducks. It was there, and the team was ready, if only life were that simple. If only sports series always followed the plot for a made-for-TV movie.

Roger Neilson was watching the game on TV from his home when the Devils scored late in the third period of a game seven that appeared on its way to overtime. With just 2:14 remaining, Jeff Friesen scored the goal that would lift the Devils into the final, where they would again lift the Cup.

Nate Bedford was with Roger when the horn sounded on the final game of his life. According to Bedford, Roger bowed his head, tears running down his cheeks and off his face. He got up from his chair and went to bed.

Bedford says he tried to get Roger to eat something.

"I can't eat tonight, Snake," he said.

It was a harsh ending, not only because the Senators had failed to win Neilson a Cup after getting so close, but also because Roger knew it was over for him. His last game by his last team.

A touch that put tears in many eyes was the year-end announcement by the Senators that Neilson and the rest of the coaching staff would be back next season. Management knew there was no chance Roger would be able to make it, but did what they could to give him hope.

"It was," says Nancy, "over and above what they needed to do."

In this sense, as in so many others, Ottawa was a wonderful final stop on the merry-go-round of Neilson's career. Nancy likes to say, "It all worked out for Roger because he ended up in Ottawa."

Three months later, when the Senators and the rest of the NHL set out on the 2003-04 season, it was the first time in twenty-six years that it started without Roger Neilson.

Leaving Them in His Dust

As per his wishes, Roger was cremated. His ashes are about as well travelled and storied as the transient coach himself. To name a few final resting places: his grave, other parts of Canada, the United States, Africa . . . the commissioner's scalp . . . yes, really.

Whether or not it was in Roger's will that his remains become the source of practical jokes, Nancy Nichols, the love of Roger's life, took it upon herself to make them so. She especially wanted to get Colin Campbell, NHL VP in his day job, The Joker in his spare time. Campbell has gone to great lengths to torture his friends, Roger included. Perhaps most famously, he sent a letter to Greg Millen on Pittsburgh Penguins stationery, informing the then-young goaltender that his first professional team would not be renewing his contract. This was days before Millen's wedding. Millen believed the letter was authentic. He and his wife-to-be

spent three tortured days sorting out their future before Campbell finally fessed up. Then, on the day of the wedding, Campbell cut off the heels of Millen's shoes.

Nancy set out to pay him back at Roger's memorial, a huge outdoor affair, more like a fall fair, with well over a thousand people in attendance. With no shortage of accomplices, she filled an urn, not with Roger's remains but with wood ash from the bonfires at the cottage in the days leading up to the memorial. Nancy approached Campbell and held out the urn.

"I know this is gonna seem weird, but Roger wanted his ashes to be put in the NHL office," she said. "I've got it in writing."

Campbell took the urn, said okay, then caught the look on the face of Buffalo Sabres coach Lindy Ruff, about to explode with laughter.

"Nice try," said Campbell.

Then it was on to the next victim. Colin's wife, Heather.

She was handed the urn, but by now the ashes were leaking through a hole in the bottom of the urn and she was in tears thinking that Roger's remains were escaping in a sooty mess all over her dress. She had to be consoled and enlightened.

Nothing like a good cremation gag.

"It was botched, but we tried, and we thought Roger would think it was funny," says Nancy.

She had only just begun. Roger was pretty good at jabbing Gary Bettman, the tiny perfect commissioner. One of Neilson's most famous quotes was the one about the two things you don't want to know: "what's inside a hot dog and what goes on inside the NHL office."

Her resolve perhaps strengthened by a couple of glasses of wine, Nancy used the occasion of Bettman's visit to the Corel Centre at the opening of the 2003-04 season to play a little joke on him. Bettman was there as part of a tribute to Roger. The Senators season was being dedicated in his honour. Up in the suite, watching

the game, Nancy snuck up behind the commish, dumped some of Roger's ashes in his hair, and said, "Now Roger's gonna be in your hair forever."

The rest of Roger's remains met with more conventional passage. Nancy has some with her in Dallas. She saved some for Dallas Eakins and his family. Eakins, who was probably the closest professional player to Roger, went to Hawaii with Darren Keily, armed with a small pack of ashes to distribute around the Neilson gang's annual vacation destination for sixteen years or so.

Eakins was anxious to free the ashes from their pouch, or at least thought Neilson would be anxious about it. "They were in this purple velour bag," says Eakins with distaste. "Almost like a purse. Roger would hate it."

Among the Maui resting places for Roger:

1. The first tee of the Plantation Course at Kapalua. "We'd tee off there at 6:00 a.m. and the view is unbelievable," says Eakins.
2. The golf course ravine where Neilson would spend half his vacation digging golf balls out of the mud.
3. On the beach behind the Nohonani resort condos, the only place Roger stayed in Maui. Blue Robinson, the resort manager and friend to Roger, joined Eakins and Keily in placing the ashes.
4. At the Hyatt Hotel, the swank place down the road, where Roger's gang would sneak in and enjoy the facilities.

Maui is a quieter island since Neilson's passing.

"I loved him," says Blue Robinson. "How could you not love him? He was here when he was taking this cancer medication, thalidomide, and he says, 'Well, Blue, there's no sex this year, says so right here on the bottle.' And he laughs.

"I miss him. But I say hi to him every day – I tap his little bob-blehead doll."

He's finally settled, Roger.

Just not in one place.

Which is perfect.

A part of him is in Toronto, part on his precious lake near Peterborough, part of him is with hockey people, part in Maui, and a part in Africa.

"I went to Bulawayo," says Nichols. "I thought I should take him back to where his mother was born, complete some sort of spiritual circle. He made a point, when they went to Africa, of going there, because he wanted to see where his mother was born, so I thought that was something he would really like. And I went to Victoria Falls, where he did his bungee jump that he bragged about forever. . . . I stood in that place where the guys were bungee jumping and I threw his ashes right there."

Of course, there are also ashes in the ground at Westminster Cemetery in north Toronto, in the Neilson family plot just a few miles from the old homestead. The burial ceremony, held about a month after the memorial, was low key to the point of being off the radar screen for many of Roger's associates. Certainly, more people, had they known about it, would have liked to attend. No more than a dozen friends were there, from Toronto and Peterborough. Nancy flew up from Dallas. After she deposited some remains into the grave of Roger Paul Neilson, Nancy scooped some dirt from the ground for safekeeping. She's hopelessly sentimental.

"I still have the last paper he ever folded for me," she says. "He refolded every newspaper he ever read. Last day in Ottawa, he folded the paper and handed it to me. And I just kept it. It sits beside my bed."

Roger's passing was especially tough on Nancy Nichols. She isn't a widow, technically, and was used to going months during the hockey season without seeing her man, but he was her man, her crazy, lovely, stubborn old man. As different as they were – he strictly religious, a teetotaller who didn't swear; she a free spirit

who drinks and curses – they were madly in love with each other.

Their differences only fuelled the attraction. Two highly intelligent, engaging people who enjoyed the challenge of a good joust. Still attractive in her early fifties, Nancy wears her blond hair at shoulder length. Hours after Roger's burial, sitting in the lounge of a Toronto hotel, she's in print slacks she picked up in Israel for five dollars. On her feet is a pair of Israeli sandals she bought when she worked at Roger's hockey camp at Metulla. A ring of twin rhinestone bands adorns one of her toes. At a glance, it looks like a diamond wedding ring worn on her foot instead of her hand.

"I'm just an old hippie trying to fit in," she says, in an accent she describes as "Texan-Canadian."

Fitting in is harder minus her other half.

"I feel like a boulder in the middle of the Colorado River when the snow is melting. All this water is coming down on the boulder, and some big chunk of me just fell off. After the funeral, I said, I don't have a team for the first time.

"I've never grown up either. I love to travel, just like Roger. I have friends all over. One of the reasons we stuck together for so long was that we both had the same mindset of, let's play. . . .

"I feel I got more out of Roger than anybody. A lot of guys wouldn't agree with that. I got a lot of the soft side of Roger, that he rarely let out."

If Roger Neilson was blushing over the honours that rained down on him in his final year – a thousand games as a head coach, the tribute dinner, Hall of Fame induction, all-star trip – the rain became a torrent after his passing.

In Peterborough, city council named a street in his honour, Roger Neilson Way, right next to the arena in which his hockey

legend was launched. Cops for Cancer, the annual campaign to raise funds for cancer research, dedicated their 2003 drive to Neilson.

In Saskatchewan, where Neilson visited a Bible school camp each summer despite grumbling about the high cost of reaching Regina, an arena was named in his honour.

Neilson's final three hockey connections in Ontario, the Senators, Peterborough Petes, and Lindsay Muskies, all wore patches on their sweaters during the season after his death featuring Roger's signature on an oval background next to a couple of bold neckties.

The Senators knew they wanted to honour Neilson in a more lasting way, something beyond the dedication of the 2003-04 season to his name, beyond the artistic Roger patch, beyond the Roger Neilson coaches booth high atop the Corel Centre.

Roy Mlakar, the club's CEO and president, sat down with Senators Foundation president Dave Ready and discussed a plan to link Roger's name with something tied to the future, not the past. Something connected with a youth initiative, for nothing could be more appropriate for the lifelong hockey coach and youth missionary.

The Senators knew a model already existed for the kind of facility they had in mind: Canuck Place Children's Hospice, a Vancouver Canucks creation that cares for children, and the families of children, with life-limiting illnesses.

Fortunately, the mental sketch of Ottawa's plan was far enough along that Mlakar was able to share the idea with Roger in person, weeks before he died. Neilson was thrilled. And so the concept of Roger's House was born, a palliative care facility to be built on the grounds of the Children's Hospital of Eastern Ontario, in Ottawa's east end.

"Every day I get donations from people who met Roger or saw Roger or know what we're doing and want to contribute because he

touched their lives in some way," says Chad Schella, director of community and corporate relations for the Senators Foundation and friend of Roger since 1985, when he was playing high school hockey in Peterborough and started working at Neilson's hockey school.

The donations come by mail, over the phone, in person. There was the guy from South Carolina who had met Roger in an airport. "Send me forty Roger pins and hats," he said, firing off a cheque for eight hundred dollars.

"That's a five-minute conversation Roger had with someone," says Schella, "and he's never forgotten it."

A female student of Roger's from Bayview Junior High in north Toronto sent up a collage of pictures of the man she'd known as "Coach," along with donations from other former students.

A gentleman who didn't want his name made public told the story of his handicapped son, in need of a wheelchair when the family didn't have the means to buy one. Roger had heard about the family and sent them a thousand dollars along with a note to say he didn't want anything back and hoped the money would help.

The man did return the thousand dollars, years later, in a cheque made out to Roger's House. "My son has his wheelchair," wrote the man, "and we're a bit better off now. Please put this toward Roger's House."

Each day, Schella is on goosebump watch for stories like these. People from all over have their personal versions of Roger's generosity and humour.

People who can't afford to help financially have promised to volunteer at the facility once it's built. There's the security guard at the Corel Centre who bought one of the limited-edition Tony Harris portraits of Roger through the Senators payroll deduction plan. The guys at the command centre were forever helping out Roger when he lost his keys or committed some other Roger-ism. They were touched when they came to work one day to find a

crate of Florida oranges; sick as he was, Neilson had sent them from the NHL all-star game.

Neilson had dinner one time at the family home of the one of the guards. "You don't know what this will mean, having this [portrait] hanging in my house," the man told Schella.

Not many know about Schella's eighteen-year association with Neilson, which has its blessings. It means they want to impress upon him how important Roger was to them, how special this campaign should be for the Foundation. Just in case Schella is not aware.

When the Senators and Ottawa 67's lost the bid to bring the World Junior Hockey Championships to Ottawa, those who had given twenty-five-dollar-ticket pledges had the option of transferring the money to Roger's House. When nearly a thousand people did, Schella sat down to personally sign 975 thank-you notes.

It was the Roger touch. Schella knew what it meant to receive a note from Neilson. He knew, as well, that Roger didn't approve of shortcuts in the well-worn path of excellence he journeyed in his life.

"To be working on this project in his memory means the world to me," says Schella.

In the first year of fundraising, more than a million dollars was raised toward the three million needed to build Roger's House, scheduled to be completed before the end of 2005. An unnamed widow has pledged an additional five hundred thousand dollars from her estate. Major corporate sponsors have come on board, and the project has become the focus of multiple charity events, including golf tournaments and the annual *Ottawa Citizen* Walk, Roll and Run for Roger, which is building into a significant September event on the community calendar.

It's beyond remarkable how the pieces have fallen into place after Roger's passing, as though guided by his hand. The Roger's House project directed by one of Roger's Boys. Darren Keily, whose life Neilson lovingly guided, lands in Peterborough as an assistant coach/assistant GM of Neilson's beloved Petes. And the Petes new

head coach? Why it's none other than Dick Todd, the former Petes coach. As a ten-year-old boy Todd tried out for Roger's baseball team and found a way of life, and now another of life's little twists has brought him home to the junior hockey team still marked with Neilson's fingerprints.

Through them all, his disciples, friends, associates, through the game and Roger's House, Neilson's legacy is safe. The spirit of the man will be captured. The stories retold.

What was it that made Roger Neilson unique among the men of hockey? The ability to stand above the predictable trappings of professional sport. To see a bigger picture. To thumb a nose occasionally.

Roger not only guided the lives of young friends and acquaintances, he let us live a hockey dream vicariously through him. By staying a child, avoiding parental and adult responsibilities, Roger didn't lose the child's appreciation for sport, its delicious perks and peculiarities. He was, forever, the boy who snuck into Leafs games by hiding out in the washroom of Maple Leaf Gardens. He slid into the red seats of that hockey shrine and took us – wide-eyed – with him.

Above all, Roger's gift was the ability to be his rumpled self in a game long since lost to the elite. He went barefoot to a banquet of suits. Friend to the friendless, he was an iconoclast to the very last.

There was a rare spark about Roger, one we all felt when he came into a room. The spark was never more apparent than when he spoke at his Hall of Fame induction about the joy of a boy and the game.

"When I was five years old, my family actually lived out on the island, Ward's Island, and I was just looking out my hotel window yesterday at the ferry boat coming in," said Roger. "The Ward's boat is the one boat where they put some vehicles on it, but this time the deck was empty, and there were six kids playing ball

hockey on the deck, pylons set up for nets, and they were having a great game all the way across the harbour.

"To me, that's Toronto, and that's Canada. It's hockey, and I wish Ken Danby had seen it. He'd have made a great painting of that."

Roger Neilson' Season-By-Season NHL Career

Head Coaching Record

Season	Club	Regular Season				Playoffs		
		GC	W	L	T	GC	W	L
1977-78	Toronto	80	41	29	10	13	6	7
1978-79	Toronto	80	34	33	13	6	2	4
1980-81	Buffalo	80	39	20	21	8	4	4
1981-82	Vancouver	5	4	0	1	17	11	6
1982-83	Vancouver	80	30	35	15	4	1	3
1983-84	Vancouver	48	17	26	5	-	-	-
	Los Angeles	28	8	17	3	-	-	-
1989-90	NY Rangers	80	36	31	13	10	5	5
1990-91	NY Rangers	80	36	31	13	6	2	4
1991-92	NY Rangers	80	50	25	5	13	6	7
1992-93	NY Rangers	40	19	17	4	-	-	-
1993-94	Florida	84	33	34	17	-	-	-
1994-95	Florida	48	20	22	6	-	-	-
1997-98	Philadelphia	21	10	9	2	5	1	4
1998-99	Philadelphia	82	37	26	19	6	2	4
1999-00	Philadelphia	82	45	25	12	18	11	7
2001-02	Ottawa	2	1	1	0	-	-	-
16 seasons		1,000	460	381	159	106	51	55

Other NHL Positions

Buffalo Sabres (1979-80)
Served as the assistant to head coach Scotty Bowman.

Vancouver Canucks (1981-82)
Served as assistant to head coach Harry Neale before assuming head coaching duties for the final five games of the regular season and the post-season.

Edmonton Oilers (1984)
Contracted as a video analyst for the Oilers during the 1984 play-offs as the team went on to capture its first of four Stanley Cups.

Chicago Blackhawks (1984-87)
Served as the assistant to head coach Orval Tessier for one season before Tessier was replaced by Bob Pulford prior to the 1985-86 season.

Assisted Pulford for two seasons before assuming duties as a pro scout for Chicago during the 1987-88 and 1988-89 seasons.

St. Louis Blues (1995-98)
Joined the Blues as assistant to head coach and GM Mike Keenan.

Assisted rookie head coach Joel Quenneville for two seasons before accepting head coaching duties with the Philadelphia Flyers.

Ottawa Senators (2000-02)
Assisted head coach Jacques Martin.

From "An Evening with Roger," program produced for the Roger Neilson testimonial dinner, 2002. Reproduced with permission.

Amateur Teams Coached by Roger Neilson, 1951-77

1951-52 Dave's White Rose hockey team

1952-53 Ideal Welding hockey team, capturing the Bantam "B" Championship

1953-54 Shopsy's Pee Wee hockey team

1954-55 Shopsy's Pee Wee hockey team and Lake Shore Motors Juvenile hockey team

1955-56 Westlake Motors Juvenile hockey team and Leaside's bantam and minor midget teams, Westlake capturing the Toronto Hockey League's Juvenile championship

1956-57 North Toronto Grads and Leaside Rangers minor bantam teams, North Toronto finishing the season as Intermediate champions

1958 Sasco Tubes bantam baseball team, becoming Toronto City League champions

1958-59 Leaside Rangers hockey

1959 Sasco Tubes bantam baseball, Parkwood Pee Wees, and Milwaukee Midgets

1959-60 Bick's Pickles Pee Wee hockey team

1960-61 Bick's Pickles Pee Wee hockey

1961 Richardsons Midget baseball

1961-62 Aurora Bears in the OHA Jr. "B" league

1962 Richardsons Midget baseball and Toronto North Lions baseball teams

1962-63 Bick's Pickles Midget hockey team, capturing the Toronto Hockey League and Provincial championships

1963 Toronto North Lions baseball team

1963-64 Toronto North Lions Major Midget hockey team

1964	Canadian Jr. Championship baseball
1965	Richardsons Midget baseball
1965-66	Weston Dodgers Midget hockey
1966	Richardsons Midget baseball, winning All-Ontario Tournament
1966-67	Weston Dodgers Midget hockey
1967	Richardsons Midget and Juvenile baseball teams
1967-68	Peterborough Petes, OHA
1968-69	Peterborough Petes
1969-70	Peterborough Petes
1970	Keene Expos Juvenile baseball team, becoming Juvenile Ontario Baseball Champions
1970-71	Peterborough Petes
1971	Keene Expos baseball
1971-72	Peterborough Petes
1972	Keene Expos
1972-73	Peterborough Petes
1973	Keene Expos
1973-74	Peterborough Petes
1974	Keene Expos
1974-75	Peterborough Petes
1975	Keene Expos
1975-76	Peterborough Petes
1976-77	Dallas Blackhawks
1977	NHL bound

From "An Evening with Roger," program produced for the Roger Neilson testimonial dinner, 2002. Reproduced with permission.

Acknowledgements

Foremost, I want to thank authors Roy MacGregor and Lawrence (we call him Larry) Scanlan. I could not have written this book without their guidance and inspiration.

Nancy Nichols was exceedingly generous with her unique insights into Roger Neilson.

There are too many Roger's Boys to name, but thanks to all of you for recounting your remarkable encounters with Roger. The parents of Todd Ervin – Lynn and Nate – spoke openly and with grace about Todd's tragic death and his special place in Roger's life.

The Ottawa Senators – management, staff, and players – were a constant help on this project. In particular, Chad Schella of the Senators Foundation and Roger's House went out of his way to help. The drive to build a palliative care facility in Roger's name is in good hands.

The somewhat beleaguered operators of Roger Neilson's Hockey Camp opened their doors for my lengthy visit and shared stories and archived material. Special thanks to operations manager Marshall Starkman.

Ron Ellis and the rest of the staff at the Hockey Hall of Fame embraced the idea of a book on Roger and opened the vault to their materials.

Among the books used as reference tools in my research were: *Towels, Triumph and Tears*, by Tony Gallagher and Mike Gasher; *Messier*, by Jeff Z. Klein; *Behind the Bench*, by Dick Irvin; *Inside Maple Leaf Gardens: The Rise and Fall of the Toronto Maple Leafs*, by William Houston. As always, Dan Diamond's *Total Hockey* was a requisite desk-side companion. Archives from *The Hockey News, Sports*

Illustrated, and various newspapers were vital. The *Peterborough Examiner* has done a nice job of following the Neilson story through the years.

Thanks to the gifted sportswriters and broadcasters who have covered Roger's teams, from Peterborough, Toronto, Vancouver, Buffalo, New York, Philadelphia, Florida, Ottawa, and other places among his many hockey stops. I am grateful to my colleagues and managers at the *Ottawa Citizen* for their assistance and fellowship.

Alex Schultz, senior editor at McClelland & Stewart, and copy editor Peter Buck, on one of his final M&S projects, were thorough, patient, and consistent with their tough love during the editing process.

At home, there were no worries. My boys, Connor and Liam, displayed uncommon respect for the closed office door. Their mother, my wife, Anne, did not waver in her commitment to supporting and encouraging this project. My gift is my family.

Finally, thanks to Roger Neilson for being a remarkable subject to explore.

Index

on Roger and Senators, 183, 197
on Roger's bungee jump, 173
on Roger's death, 198-201
on Roger's firing from Panthers, 128
on Roger's illness, 135-37
on Roger's lifestyle, 57-58, 126, 146
on Roger's newspaper expertise, 26
on Roger's travels, 168-69
relationship with Roger, 101-2, 123-25, 201-2
Niedermayer, Rob, 122, 125
Nilan, Chris, 114
Nill, Jim, 75

Oakley, Larry, 31
O'Connell, Mike, 51
Ogrodnick, John, 114
O'Malley, Terry "Mo," 25
Ontario Hockey Association/League, 10, 35, 53, 84
O'Reilly, Terry, 173
Oshawa Generals, 43, 45
Ottawa 67's, 205
Ottawa Citizen Walk, Roll and Run for Roger, 205
Ottawa Senators
after Roger's death, 199, 203
coached by Roger, 73, 75, 90, 97, 103, 138, 146, 163-64, 181-85, 187-97
formed, 121-22
rise under Martin, 182

Ottawa Senators Foundation, 149, 203-5

Palmateer, Mike, 54
Peacock, Doug, 23, 28, 40, 143, 164
Pearce, Kent
on-ice instructor, 14-15
on Roger and Clarke, 135
on Roger's driving, 89
on Roger's golfing, 92-93
on Roger's quirks, 101
on Roger's travels, 89, 164, 171-74
Pearce, Susan, 4, 102, 106, 171
Pearce, Tom, 15, 41, 89, 106, 173
Pearn, Perry, 97, 184-85, 191, 194
Pearson, Larry
camp supervisor, 8-9
one of Roger's Boys, 38, 145-47, 149
on Roger's driving, 91
on Roger's hockey camps, 13-14
Roger's executor, 8, 11
Pellowe, John, 23
Pelyk, Mike, 51
Perras, Mark, 46
Perreault, Gilbert, 65-66, 109
Peterborough Petes
after Roger's death, 203
coached by Bowman, ix
coached by Keily, 150, 157, 205